SUCCESSFUL INVESTMENT

SUCCESSFUL INVESTMENT

MALCOLM CRAIG

London
GEORGE ALLEN & UNWIN
Boston   Sydney

First published in 1979

GEORGE ALLEN & UNWIN LTD
40 Museum Street, London, WC1A 1LU

© Malcolm Craig 1979

British Library Cataloguing in Publication Data

Craig, Malcolm
  Successful Investment.
  1. Investments – Great Britain
  I. Title
  332.6'78'0941   HG5435   78–40851

ISBN 0–04–332069–4

Typeset in 11 on 12pt Times by Unwin Brothers Limited
and printed in Great Britain by The Gresham Press, Old Woking, Surrey

DEDICATION

To Fiona, Louise and Simon

CONTENTS

Tables

Figures

Preface

After some two decades in the City of London, there must
have been many men and women concerned with the investment of money – stockbrokers and jobbers, institutional investment fund managers and bankers, financial journalists and
money market dealers – who have assisted me in the prepa-
ration of this book. Conversations, whether over a meal, or
over a chance meeting in one of the City's bustling thorough-
fares or crowded alleyways, or over the telephone, have provided innumerable pieces of valuable information. Added to
these helpers are the many hundreds of readers who have
written to me as a result of an article or broadcast in which
I have attempted to marshal all the facts and to present them,
warts and all, to those interested in a particular sector of the
investment markets. I am grateful to all of them.

While it is not practical for me to thank by name all my
helpers, it would be ungrateful of me not to single out a
number of contributors whose assistance has been invaluable.
Geoffrey Dutton, Investment Director of Lazard Bros & Co.,
made detailed and constructive criticisms and suggestions on
all the early chapters of *Successful Investment* which relate
to investment in ordinary shares, whether direct or through
the medium of unit or investment trusts. My former employers,
Samuel Montagu, provided valuable help and information on
both the UK and overseas stock markets and, being members
of the London Gold Market and the London Silver Market,
were of great assistance in the chapters dealing with investment
in 'bullion' gold coins and in silver. The Hon. David Montagu,
who was Chairman of Samuel Montagu when I made my daily
trip to the bank's headquarters in Old Broad Street, and who
is now Chairman of Orion Bank, first introduced me to the
mysteries of the investment trust world – having pioneered the

introduction of 'split level' investment trusts in the UK. My former colleagues Bryan Hawkins and Robert Colville, both directors of Samuel Montagu, were both most helpful with advice and guidance on gilt-edged investment.

I acknowledge with gratitude the information and help provided by the Stock Exchange, by the Unit Trust Association, and by Charles Potts, a partner in Tilling & Co. (Stockbrokers), by the Association of Investment Trust Companies in those chapters dealing with investment in shares both through the Stock Exchange direct or through the intermediary of a unit trust, or by investing in shares in an investment trust. I also thank Michael Prag, the partner in charge of research at stockbrokers Simon & Coates, together with a number of his colleagues, for their help over the technicalities of rights issues and convertibles.

It is largely due to the help of stockbrokers Sternberg, Thomas Clarke & Co., who have particular expertise in options and warrants markets, that I have been able to explain the workings of these somewhat volatile markets simply and, I trust, lucidly. The monitoring service over the warrants market provided by *Investors Bulletin* has also been most helpful.

Others to whom I am indebted for help with the chapters on investment in shares, both here in the UK and overseas, are Messrs Phillips & Drew, stockbrokers, Jim Nichols, Deputy Chairman of the Britannia Group of Investment Companies, N. Kagami, Manager and Senior Economist of the Nomura Research Institute in London, and T. Yoshimura the Director and General Manager of the Portfolio Investment Department at the Tokyo Head Office of Nomura Securities – one of Japan's biggest investment dealing and banking houses.

The local authority world is an often neglected investment market and I am indebted to both Mr W.L. Dixon, a Director of Buxton's & MMB Ltd, local authority money brokers, and to Helene Gross, Principal Dealer, Co-ordinator, at the Chartered Institute of Public Finance and Accountancy Loans Bureau, for their consistent and continuing help.

I thank the Building Societies Association, Joanna Slaughter of *The Observer* (whose weekly column in the financial pages of that Sunday newspaper deserves wider recognition) and the

National Savings Movement for their combined help with respect to the relevant chapters.

Gerry Barker and Richard Worthington, Directors of sterling and foreign exchange dealers Astley & Pearce (itself a subsidiary of discount house Gerrard & National), Michael Warren, Managing Director of M.W. Marshall (Sterling Brokers) and Roy Harris of Saturn Investments Ltd have all helped me to familiarise myself with, and to explain to others, the workings of the somewhat arcane world of the money markets and money funds. For help with commodity markets I thank M.L. Doxford & Co., leading commodity brokers, Lawrence Banks, Investment Director of the Save & Prosper Group and Mark St Giles, Managing Director of Allied Hambros.

In writing on gold coins I am most appreciative of the help provided by Guy Field, Director of Derby & Co., by Samuel Montagu's *Annual Bullion Review*, by Spink & Son and by coin expert Robin Blackmore. The investment diamond market – despite the latent fire of this particular investment – holds a number of problems for the unwary, and in investigating the diamond market I am indebted to Diamond Investors & Manufacturers AG of Antwerp, and also to *Money Which*. In looking into the silver market I was assisted by two publications – Samuel Montagu's *Monthly Silver Report*, the *Annual Bullion Review* – and also by information provided by the London Metal Exchange.

For providing the raw material necessary to write the chapters on investment in agricultural land and in woodland I am grateful for the facts and figures provided by the Ministry of Agriculture, Fisheries and Food, the Investment & Economics Department of the Economic Forestry Group, The Forestry Commission, the Timber Trade Federation of the United Kingdom and the Country Landowners Association. Caroline Bosly, hand-made carpet broker, and Jack Franses, carpet consultant to Sotheby's, provided most useful information and guidance when I investigated the investment potential of hand-made carpets.

Last, but by no means least, I thank my wife Jill, without whose continued help and encouragement *Successful Investment* would not have been written.

Introduction

To many, 'investment' means buying and selling shares in quoted UK companies. To others, investment means putting their stock of capital into a secure, income-producing home. There are also those to whom investment provides the excitement of the gambling table or the race track, who consequently seek the more volatile investment markets, such as commodities. And, particularly during this age of uncertainty in which the erosive effects of inflation have touched everyone with the brush of fear, there are many who seek to place part of their wealth in tangible assets – coins, stamps, land – which may keep pace with, or even outpace, the rate of inflation. *Successful Investment* is designed to cater for all these audiences.

However, the requirements of each man or woman when it comes to deploying their free capital to best advantage among the bewildering array of investment markets open to them, are different. Everyone's individual circumstances differ, even if only marginally. The company executive or the professional man, receiving a highly taxed salary, will clearly not seek to add unearned income which is subject not only to his highest marginal rate of tax, but also, depending on the amount of unearned income involved, to the investment income surcharge. In such a situation, the most attractive investment strategy is likely to be to seek capital gain, which attracts a much lower rate of tax than does unearned income. Even the capital-gain seeker, however, needs to maintain a reserve cushion of cash in case the market turns against him, or in case an unanticipated investment opportunity suddenly presents itself. This reserve should be invested in an easily accessible and secure home, but not left sitting idly on current account with a clearing bank.

1

Other investors – perhaps the bulk of them – prefer to take the middle road. For example, a retired couple living on a pension may well have built up some capital, perhaps from the sale of a bigger house which they now no longer need, perhaps from maturing insurance policies. With a less onerous tax burden than the high income earner, the investment strategy of such a couple may well be to increase their capital by means of a prudent investment policy, in order to leave their children or grandchildren a nest-egg. They may also look to that capital sum to produce income with which to augment their pension. For them, a mixture of low-risk capital gain, allied to reasonable income, is a sensible aim.

At the furthest end of the investment spectrum from the latter group is the true speculator – the 'in and out' operator who seeks spectacular capital gains and is prepared to take the risk of commensurate losses. Such an investor is more likely to focus on the commodities investment markets, which produce no income but only the chance of a capital gain or loss. Or he may prefer the heady excitements offered by the options or warrants markets. In the case of the investor who gambles in the commodities markets, tax is something of a grey area. His gains may be taxed as capital, or as income, depending on whether he is judged to be an investor or a trader. Decisions can vary from one tax office to another. For those seeking capital gain from what, for want of a better phrase, I shall call the 'traditional' investment markets (encompassing share and gilt investment), chapters 1 to 9 will prove most rewarding. These chapters take the reader through investment in ordinary shares in the UK stock market and the investment opportunities offered by overseas stock markets, and end with a study of the investment opportunities offered by the gilt-edged (or Government) stock market.

Sandwiched between the chapters dealing with investment in ordinary shares in the UK and investment in gilt-edged stock are included a number of chapters dealing with aspects of share investment with which the reader should familiarise himself if he is to become a successful investor. These chapters explain and advise on rights issues, the use of the options and the warrants markets and how to evaluate convertible loan stocks.

For those seeking the peace of mind of the managed fund – that peace of mind which can come from handing over the responsibility of making investment decisions to others – I have included two chapters evaluating investment through both unit trusts and investment trusts.

While I have attempted to highlight both the opportunities and the pitfalls of each investment market in turn, I have in the interests of clarity left out some points of finer detail (not wishing to be accused of taking the reader to that dubious vantage point from which he can see the trees but not the wood). For those seeking information over and above that contained in the first section of the book, the following names and addresses will prove useful: the Stock Exchange, London EC2; the Unit Trust Association, 16 Finsbury Circus, London EC2; the Association of Investment Trust Companies, 16 Finsbury Circus, London EC2. Behind each of these organisations lies an infrastructure of other help – from stockbrokers, unit trust, and investment trust, management companies and others too numerous to list here – to whom the enquirer will be directed. Indeed, the Stock Exchange is anxious to encourage the private investor to return in greater numbers to a stock market which has become increasingly dominated by institutional investment fund managers – a development which is giving cause for concern.

For those seeking income, chapters 10 to 13 will be of most interest because they explain the investment possibilities created by the borrowing needs of Britain's five hundred or so local authorities. A detailed survey is also carried out on the investment market provided by the now vast building society movement, which has overtaken Britain's banking community as a home for deposit funds. Chapters on the National Savings movement and on the workings of the money markets and the money funds have also been included. The latter – the money markets and the money funds – are the least familiar of all the income-producing sectors to the private investor, but they are worthy of comment as they do from time to time offer high and riskless income-earning opportunities. Those seeking more information than is contained in these chapters would be well advised to contact: the Chartered Institute of Public Finance and Accountancy, 1 Buckingham Place, London SW1, and at the CIPFA Loans Bureau, 232 Vauxhall Bridge Road, London SW1; the Building Societies Association, 14 Park Street, London, W1; the National Savings Movement, Alexandra House, Kingsway, London WC2.

For those seeking more detailed knowledge of the workings of the money markets there is no central reference point. With some diffidence, therefore, I am forced to draw the reader's attention to the existence of my own book, *The Sterling Money Markets*, published by Gower Press, which has become something of a standard work in this field.

When it comes to commodity investment (chapters 14 and 15) I must emphasise yet again that this is an investment sector for the true speculator. The rewards can be great but so can the losses. There is no central point to which I can direct the reader wishing to know more about direct investment in commodities or about investment via the off-shore commodity funds. However, for those seeking the lowest-risk approach to commodity investment – through the commodity unit trusts – the Unit Trust Association will be able to provide advice and guidance.

Chapters 16 to 21 deal with the non-traditional investment sectors (sometimes called inflation hedges) which offer no income but only the chance of capital gain – coins, diamonds, silver, stamps and hand-made carpets. I have included only those markets where reliable data exists (such as prices fetched at auction sales), and I have stopped short of trying to assess the investment merits of particular inflation hedges for which reliable data does not exist. I have found, as I am sure the interested reader will also find, that the appropriate experts at the great London auction houses have proved unfailingly helpful. I list these houses, together with a lady carpet broker who proved to be a mine of information on her particular market: Sotheby & Co, 34 New Bond Street, London W1; Christies, 8 King Street, London SW1; Phillips, 7 Blenheim Street, London W1; Caroline Bosly (Oriental carpet broker), 13 Princess Road, London NW1.

When it comes to investment in land – agricultural or woodland – there is always investment interest. Land provides income, capital gain, a view and certain tax advantages. Useful addresses are:

The Ministry of Agriculture, Fisheries and Food, Whitehall Place, London SW1;
The Economic Forestry Group, 26 Old Bailey, London EC4;
The Forestry Commission, 25 Savile Row, London W1;
The Timber Trade Federation of the UK, Clareville House, Whitcomb Street, London WC2;
The Country Landowners Association, 16 Belgrave Square, London SW1.

Lastly, and I say this somewhat tongue in cheek, on matters of tax, I have often found it both cheaper and easier to obtain correct information from the original fount itself rather than from a tax consultant, accountant or solicitor. My source has been, and is: The Inland Revenue, Somerset House, Strand, London WC2.

I am always interested to know what my readers think on all the investment markets I monitor. From them I gain some excellent nuggets of information which deserve a wider audience. I will take the nuggets along with the inevitable brickbats. Write to me with either at Birchwood, Dukes Ride, Gerrards Cross, Bucks., or at my office at 5th floor, 38 Berkeley Square, London W1.

Chapter 1

Successful Investment in Ordinary Shares

It is interesting to reflect that, as all markets move in cycles, the market in UK ordinary shares may have returned to the position it occupied in the mid-fifties. At that time, respectable investors both private and corporate were not at all enchanted with ordinary shares as an investment. A modest holding of blue chips, certainly, but the British then were much more Government-stock-oriented. It was the Church Commissioners – or rather the committee which looked after the Church of England's finances – which first saw the possibilities offered by ordinary shares as a means of maintaining and increasing the real value of the capital under their management.

During the late 'fifties and throughout the 'sixties there was a stampede into ordinary shares, a stampede to which even greater momentum was given by the cash pouring into the institutional funds managers' hands as the British became more pension and insurance conscious. Investors were prepared to accept a lower income, in the form of a dividend, from their ordinary shareholdings than was obtainable from medium and long-term Government stocks – a psychological attitude which became encapsulated in the phrase 'the reverse yield gap'. The reasoning behind investment in ordinary shares was that the shareholder had a stake in a company which actually made things or provided services, and the price at which these could be sold would inevitably keep pace with inflation. Shares offered the chance of capital gain, and there was the additional sweetener for the high income tax payer that capital gains were for many years tax free, and even when capital gains tax was imposed, it was at a much lower rate than income tax.

7

These benefits more than outweighed the risks of ordinary share investment and so the equity cult held sway for almost twenty years.

In 1974 the bubble was pricked when a quadrupling of oil prices, banana republic levels of inflation and industrial strife in the UK, plus a worldwide recession, caused the *Financial Times* 30-share index to plummet to 146, as against its previous high, reached in the spring of 1972, of 542. Haggard stockbrokers in that miserable winter of 1974 laid off staff in their hundreds, and those that were left spoke of the merits of investing in gold coins, silver bar, (even, and only half-jokingly) tins of baked beans – anything in fact which could possibly survive as a store of value as the Apocalypse approached. Like all things to do with investment, which is an action primarily impelled by greed and fear and without much logic to it, the slide was overdone.

A few astute investment managers started buying cheaply in January 1975, when Britain's best blue-chip share, ICI, was yielding a fat 14.6 per cent. Other professionals, with mountains of cash sitting on the money markets, were anxious not to be left behind. In one heady day in February the index leaped nearly 20 points, and from a low of 146 reached 300 inside three months. By 14 September 1977 the index reached a new peak of 549.2.

THE LESSONS OF EXPERIENCE

What can we learn from the experience of the last ten years? Most investors, or rather most private investors, buy ordinary shares and sit on them for long periods of time. In a bull market they open the Saturday edition of the *Financial Times* to see how their ordinary shareholding prices are progressing and congratulate themselves on how well they are doing, and then worry about wealth tax and capital transfer tax. In a bear market they watch the value of their shares go down with a sinking heart or, if the bear market is sufficiently vicious as was the case in 1974, they either do not look at share prices at all or sell in a blind panic while they can still get something for their shares. But, on the whole, private investors do not buy and sell shares regularly. The 'market makers' are the professional investment managers whose job it is to buy and sell at something approaching the right time. That, after all, is what they are paid for. However, if the shareholder looks back over his shoulder to the past fifteen or sixteen years he would find that equities have been the most profitable form of investment in only six of those years. Equities provided a higher return than that from fixed interest stocks or from just leaving cash on deposit at the bank in 1963, 1965, 1967, 1968, 1972 and 1975. While equities have shown over this period a greater return overall than investment in Government stocks or cash on deposit, as an investment they still have not kept pace with the cost of living as measured by the increase in retail prices.

Fixed-interest securities, including Government (gilt-edged) stock, have been the most disappointing form of investment over the last sixteen years in that they have shown up as the best performer in two years only – 1962 and 1976. Most surprisingly of all, just leaving your cash sitting idly on deposit has appeared the best thing to do in no less than eight of the last sixteen years – 1960, 1961, 1964, 1966, 1969, 1970, 1973, 1974. It would be very easy to conclude that it is much the best thing to put your money into a bank or building society deposit and forget about it, but the value of your capital would erode away year after year under the harsh winds of inflation. True, the value of your capital would not have been maintained had you remained fully invested in a representative selection of ordinary shares throughout the years above, but you *would* have increased the value of your capital in both nominal and real terms had you bought near the bottom of each bear market and sold out near the top.

THE IMPORTANCE OF TIMING

In 1963 you would have increased your capital by over 30 per cent. In 1967 and 1968 your shareholding would have increased in value by nearly 70 per cent in the two years. In 1971–2 the index went from the 300 level to 540, and if you had been brave enough to buy shares in December 1975 you would have seen your capital double in three months. Bear in mind also that it pays not to be greedy. You can never get out at the peak, so be prepared to take your profits as the market rises towards the peak. It is much easier to sell on a rising market than on a falling market: during the gloom and doom days of late 1974 you could not sell more than 5,000 shares in ICI – which for a wholesale share market like the UK Stock Exchange (in which the average value of *each* bargain has been around £17,000) is a ridiculously small amount. Equally, during the first heady months of 1975 you could not buy less than 5,000 ICI shares without the jobbers marking up the share price exorbitantly against such small deals.

The name of the equity investment game is flexibility. Be prepared to buy and to sell. The lessons of experience are that you lose out if you are a long-term holder.

SECTOR SWITCHING

In general terms, if you get your timing right, then (almost) anything you buy in the way of first or second-rank shares should be pulled up by a bull market climate. The blue-chip leaders tend to move first, then the professional fund managers start eyeing hungrily the differentials created between the blue chips and the second-rank shares, and this pulls up the prices of the latter. So while a bull market is in progress, if you want to maximise your profits then switch between sectors. The table below provides examples from selected years and shows just how important it is to keep an eye on different share sectors.

As individual sectors come and go into and out of fashion, major price swings take place, so close study of the market in this sort of detail does provide the astute investor with the opportunity to make more profits than on the market as a whole. It is perfectly possible to buy shares in a bull market and make a loss because they happen to be in an unpopular market sector. As the table shows, it is also possible to make money in a bear market by buying into the right sector.

Now most private investors, when it comes to choosing a share, devote all their faculties to choosing the 'right' share. Beware of this 'man in the street' mentality, the mentality that dictates that the right share to buy is, say, Marks and Spencer or ICI or Shell. If you look at the performance of some of

Table 1. *UK Share Sector Performance in Selected Years*

Year	Best performance	Worst performance	% Change in Financial Times 30-share index*
1967	+63% Electricals	−8% Rubbers	+24%
1968	+111% Merchant banks	−1% Tins	+32%
1970	+18% Gold mining shares	−63% Shipbuilding	−17%
1971	+85% Contracting and Construction industry	−14% Mining finance	+40%
1972	+105% Miscellaneous financial	+10% Rubbers	+7%
1973	+9% Rubbers	−51% Miscellaneous financial	−32%
1974	+1% Coppers	−80% Hire purchase	−53%
1975	+203% Entertainment and catering	−32% Coppers	+133%
1976	+40% Tins	−35% Merchant banks	−6%
1977	+115% Hire purchase	+11% Mining finance	+42%

*The *Financial Times* Industrial Ordinary Share Index records the price movements, in index form, of thirty leading UK industrial shares. For this reason it is referred to throughout this book as the *Financial Times* 30-share index, to avoid confusion with any other Financial Times index.

these popular shares you will find that there are many others which do better. Take the bull market in 1975. ICI went from 118 pence in January 1975 to top the 400 pence mark eventually. But other shares bettered even this jump. Among the 'exotics', for example, Cavenham warrants increased by some 500 per cent. And do not blinker your eyes to the fact that there are other share markets in the world than London − there are markets in the USA, (dealt with in chapter 8), Europe, Australia and Japan plus several others which may be going up while the UK market is going down.

THE MECHANICS OF THE MARKET PLACE

We wondered at the beginning of this chapter whether investors have returned to the attitude of the mid-fifties, an attitude

Table 2. *The Pattern of Ownership of Quoted Ordinary Shares 1963–73*

Category of ownership	1963 %	1973 %
Persons, executors and trustees of residents in UK	58.7%	42.0%
Charities etc.	2.6%	4.4%
Insurance companies	10.7%	16.2%
Pension funds	7.0%	12.2%
Investment trust companies	6.7%	6.5%
Unit trusts	1.2%	3.4%
Banks and other financial institutions	2.3%	3.3%
Non-financial companies	4.8%	4.3%
Public sector	1.6%	2.5%
Overseas	4.4%	5.2%
	100.0%	100.0%
Total market value of issued ordinary shares (£million)	£27,500	£40,520

(Source: Royal Commission on the Distribution of Income and Wealth.)

which said that ordinary shares had their place in a portfolio but were not the be all and end all of keeping your capital intact. Certainly the figures above show that private investors have become less interested in the stock market over the decade 1963–1973.

While private investors (including executors and trustees) account for a lower proportion of the share ownership market in 1973, the last year for which statistics are available, than they did in 1963, the private investor still constitutes the biggest market sector. The institutions which are normally thought of as the real powers in the share-owning world – pension funds, insurance companies, investment and unit trusts – still account for only 38 per cent of shares as against the private investors' 42 per cent (see table 2). The trouble is that the institutions are active – they buy and sell all the time – while the private investment sector is static. This means that the market place is dominated by and geared to the requirements of the institutional fund managers; this is a source of weakness as the institutions tend to move in the same direction at the same time. Stockbrokers have clipped away their private-client business over the years (although some are now regret-ting this) to become the servants of the big insurance com-panies, banks and pension funds. Provincial brokers apart, this means that the brokers will normally only take on business of the £20,000-plus variety, and even then some may resort to 'churning' (over-frequent buying and selling of shares on behalf of a client) in order to produce commission income.

CAPITAL GAINS TAX

For the higher-rate taxpayer capital gains tax, even at 30 per cent, is obviously more attractive than is income tax, hence the desire on the part of most investors for capital gain as opposed to income. In his April 1978 Budget the Chancellor introduced an exemption for individual gains up to £1,000 and reduced liability for gains between £1,000 and £9,500. For 1977–8 and for subsequent years an individual whose total net gains in a year of assessment do not exceed £1,000 is not charged capital gains tax. Where the gains do not exceed £5,000 the excess over £1,000 is charged at a reduced rate of 15 per cent. Where the gains exceed £5,000, liability is limited to tax of £600 plus half of the excess over £5,000. This marginal relief runs out at £9,500. Gains of £9,500 and more are charged at the full capital gains tax rate of 30 per cent.
  Examples of small gains relief are shown below:

a. Net gains   £2,000
    Exempt   £1,000
    Tax   £1,000@15%=£150
b. Net gains   £6,000
    Tax   £600
    +(£6,000−£5,000)×½=£500
    ─────────────────────────
    Total tax £1,100(18·3%)

Although losses incurred during the year are set off against gains from the year, losses brought forward will be used only

13

to the extent necessary to reduce gains to £1,100. An individual is not normally required to show in his tax return total chargeable gains (before losses) of £1,100 or less except where the total disposal proceeds exceed £5,000.

Chapter 2

The Unit Trust World – Good Only in Parts

There are some 396 unit trusts available to UK investors and the number of unit holder accounts (which is not to be confused with the number of unit holders) has declined by about 8 per cent since 1971 due to merger by some unit trusts, some rationalisation by investors and the conversion of holdings into equity-linked policies. The number of unit holders investing directly in unit trusts is estimated to be 1¼ million, and ¾ million invest indirectly via unit-linked policies. The value of funds managed by the unit trust industry is some £2,570 million. Every month a proportion of the units in the industry are cashed in by unit holders, and annual repurchases as a percentage of total funds have varied during the last ten years between 4 per cent and 8 per cent.

Why do unit trusts exist at all? They were formed (and continue to be formed) to offer the individual investor a chance to spread his risks by buying units, which in turn invest in a balanced portfolio of shares. In theory, this technique of 'pooling' a large number of small investors into one buying organisation – the unit trust – is marketed as being a better method of investment in ordinary shares for the smaller investor than if he goes it alone, does his own selection and buys his own shares in just a few share sectors. Additionally, the unit trust buyer gets rid of the headaches (and some of the fun) attendant on running his own investment portfolio by handing over the job and attendant paper work to the unit trust company's professional management. The assets of the

15

funds are held by independent trustees so security is reasonably assured.

TYPES OF UNIT TRUSTS

The marketing experts at the unit trusts have thought up all sorts of gimmicks over the years to attract the investing public, and they have had a fruitful background against which to work as private investors have increasingly pulled out of the stock market and as stockbrokers and investment managers have swung towards catering for the big customers like the pension funds and the insurance companies. By being so aggressive, the unit trust industry has partly cooked its own goose. Unit trusts have been formed, and advertised with large-budget advertising programmes, for every conceivable purpose, and there are now far too many of them.

Trusts have been formed to cater for those who want high income, for those who want capital gains, for those who want a combination of both, for North Sea oil, for motorway construction, for investment in firms involved in commodities trading, for investment in various stock markets overseas, and for gold investment (or rather investment in gold mining companies). You name it, the unit trust industry has (probably) thought about it.

MANAGEMENT CHARGES

'What,' you naturally ask, 'do the unit trust management companies get out of it?' In this country unit trust management companies are allowed to make a charge of 5 per cent initially (some charge 3¼ per cent) which is known in the trade as 'front-end loading'. Part of this front-end loading is available as a kickback – or, more cosmetically, 'introductory commission' – to insurance brokers, stockbrokers and recognised agents who bring business to the unit trust. In addition there is an annual management charge of ⅜ per cent (when the initial fee is 5 per cent) or ½ per cent (when the initial fee is 3¼ per cent), which is based on the value of the funds under management. These figures may not sound very much, but what it boils down to is that if you invest £10,000 in a unit

Table 3. *Best Performing Unit Trusts over One to Seven Years*

To 1 Jan 1978	Unit Trust	Value of £100 invested	Percentage gain
12 months	M & G Recovery	£217.30	+117.3
24 months	M & G Recovery	£224.50	+124.5
36 months	Framlington Income	£484.90	+384.9
48 months	Gartmore High Income	£293.30	+193.3
60 months	Barclays Unicorn Professional Assoc.	£279.20	+179.2
72 months	M+G Recovery	£314.50	+214.5
84 months	M+G Recovery	£513.80	+413.8

(Source: *Planned Savings*)

trust, as a result of the front-end loading, the value of your capital is reduced immediately to £9,500. This is all very well if the value of your capital is increased by astute investment management by more than the front-end loading and annual management charge, but relatively few unit trusts manage to beat even the *Financial Times* 30-share index. Hence the reason why the great British investing public has become increasingly disenchanted with unit trusts as a form of investment. The best performing unit trusts over periods of one to seven years are shown in table 3. As can readily be seen, M & G Recovery has come out top over four of the periods monitored by *Planned Savings*.

BID AND OFFER PRICES

The 'bid' price is the price at which the unit trust management will buy back units. The 'offer' price is the price at which the managers will sell the units. The spread between bid and offer prices varies between unit trusts; generally it is around 7 per cent which incorporates the initial fee. The bid price of the units is decided by the market value of the unit trust's shares, cash and accumulated income. The offer price is related to the market value of the unit trust's assets plus expenses.

Units in unit trusts can be bought and sold at any time: in

fact unit trusts are allowed only to invest in quoted Stock Exchange securities in order to provide unit holders with easy liquidity.

METHODS OF INVESTING IN UNIT TRUSTS

There are a variety of ways in which you can invest in unit trusts. You can either put in a lump sum, or save as you earn with monthly savings plans, or you can link regular savings plans to life insurance (with certain tax advantages). You can also exchange your existing, directly purchased shares, for units. This latter method has been pushed particularly hard as private shareholders have pulled back from direct investment in the stock market. The share exchange scheme works as follows. If you have 1,000 shares whose market bid price is 100p and whose offer price is 105p you could sell them through a broker for £1,000 less commission, contract stamp and VAT (£16.50), resulting in your receiving £983.50. However, if the shares happen to be shares which the unit trust company is prepared to add to its own portfolio (usually UK or overseas blue chips) then it will buy them from you at either half the difference between the bid price and the offer price (102½p) or at the full offer price (105p) and credit you with units to that value. But if the unit trust company does not wish to add your shares to its portfolio, it will normally sell them for you and pass on to you the full bid value in units. Bear in mind that an exchange of shares for units in a unit trust is regarded as a disposal for capital gains tax purposes.

THE TAX POSITION

At this point it is worth talking a little more about the tax position on unit trusts. So far as income tax is concerned, with each distribution of income from a unit trust the unit holder gets a voucher detailing the income and the tax credit relating to it, which together make up the income for tax purposes. The tax credit is equivalent to tax at the basic rate of tax, and no further tax is due from unit holders attracting tax at the basic rate. Unit holders with an excess of personal reliefs to set against their unit trust income can reclaim all or part of the tax credit from the Inland Revenue. Conversely, unit holders liable to tax at a higher rate or to the investment income surcharge will have additional tax to pay.

As for capital gains tax, a holding in a unit trust is a chargeable asset for CGT purposes and you have to show purchases and sales on your tax return. Unit holders disposing of their unit trust holding receive, for CGT purposes, a credit which is equivalent to half the basic rate of tax. This means that most standard-rate taxpayers pay no tax on gains made through unit trusts. The maximum credit will remain at 17 per cent until 1979–80, when it will be reduced to 10 per cent.

Where unit holders do have to pay CGT, the maximum rate in respect of unit trust holdings is currently 13½ per cent. Losses arising on the disposal of units must be offset against other gains made in the same year. Any balance remaining can be carried forward and set against gains in later years. The extra tax relief mentioned earlier in connection with unit-trust-linked insurance schemes arises from the fact that such schemes are a variation of an ordinary life insurance arrangement except that the premiums are invested in unit trusts. Their major attraction is that you can get tax relief on the premiums.

UNIT TRUST SELECTION

The overall performance of unit trusts, like the curate's egg, is good only in parts. When we said at the outset that investors, by buying units in a unit trust, were ridding themselves of the worry of making their own investment decisions, this was only partially true. The prospective unit trust buyer is still left with two crucial investment decisions. One is when to buy units in a unit trust. If he gets in at the bottom of the stock market and gets out at the top, he can still increase his capital even within the confines of an average performance unit trust. Bear in mind, though, that unit trusts see it as their job in life to remain fully invested in shares at all times, whether in the UK or overseas. So when a really vicious bear market develops, as in 1974, the unit holder is carried inexorably down as share prices slide. If he remains a private (direct) investor, and gets his timing right, then he always has the opportunity of going into cash. But because of the front-end loading involved in unit trust buying they are really long-term investments – it takes a long time for the unit trust to make up, in performance terms, the 5 per cent you lose at the outset. The lesson of history is that the average member of the investing public has tended to buy units in unit trusts when the stock market is nearing the peak of a bull market, and then starts to unload (sometimes in panic) when the market is near the bottom. This 'herd instinct' buying pattern by unit trust customers has resulted in the professionals regarding an upsurge in unit trust buying as signalling the peak of a bull market – and time to get out. Such behaviour also enables the professional to unload part of their holdings at the top end of a bull market to the unit trusts, providing them with a convenient outlet but without disturbing the market over much.

The other point to bear in mind is that long-term investment is a mug's game, whether it be in shares, gilts, commodities or unit trusts. Unless you are very lucky indeed, you cannot buy units in a unit trust (or even in a unit trust whose purpose in life is to buy units in other unit trusts) and then sit back and watch your capital increase steadily year by year. One year's star unit trust may be next year's dud, so you are still left with the problem of moving in and out of unit trusts operating in diverse fields in the UK and overseas. And the front-end loading factor each time you buy means that you are trying to pursue a successful investment policy with one arm tied behind your back.

Looking at performance tables and selecting the unit trust which tops the table can lose you your money, as evidenced by the fact that Slater Walker Gold & General topped the unit trust league in 1974, but came next to bottom in the following year. In fact you could make out quite a good argument for picking out the bottom performance in one year as a good investment for the next. Perhaps a more reliable guide might be provided by sustained performance over a period of years, which is given in table 3.

The investor still has to make the two crucial investment decisions when deciding to buy units in a unit trust. One is when to buy – and when to sell. The other is in which sector to invest.

Chapter 3

Investment Trusts – the Sleeping Giants

Investment trusts have been around a good deal longer than unit trusts. They go back over a century or more to when investment trusts were formed to channel money into projects requiring large slabs of investment capital – for example, the railway networks in the USA. In the UK they expanded steadily until 1972, the peak year for the investment trust business, when the trusts had something over £6 billion under management.

INVESTMENT TRUSTS AND UNIT TRUSTS COMPARED

The reasons why the investment trust concept is less familiar to the UK investing public are to be found in the differences between the better known (but much more recent) unit trusts and investment trusts. One major difference is that investment trusts are not allowed to advertise their wares, whereas most investors will be familiar with the large unit trust advertisements in newspapers and on billboards at railway stations. The reason for this is that an investor in an investment trust buys shares in a limited liability company, and the latter is subject to the dictates of the 1948 and 1967 Companies Acts. An investor in a unit trust, on the other hand, buys units in a trust fund authorised by the Department of Trade, and these units can be advertised at any time. The only time an investment trust company can advertise its attractions to the investing public is when it is first launched; after that initial launching only its annual results can be advertised.

Another major difference is that an investment trust company, like any other limited liability company, has a fixed amount of capital and hence the term that an investment trust is a 'close-ended fund'. The point of this is that the capital of the trust need not be increased if the conditions on the investment scene are unfavourable, such as during a bear market. Unit trusts on the other hand, are 'open-ended' and the managers of the unit trust can make available more units, or buy back existing units, whenever required by the unit holders.

While units in unit trusts are normally bought and sold through the unit trust management company, the shares of an investment trust, like any other public company, are bought and sold through the Stock Exchange. Shares of investment trust companies are bought and sold at the market price while unit trust units are bought at a price which is based on the underlying asset value plus an allowance for expenses. Investment trust companies can, like any other public company, 'gear up' (borrow money) but unit trusts can only issue 'equity units', which means they cannot borrow more money than the shareholders, or unit holders, have made available to them. In addition, investment trusts can hold back part of their earnings for further investment, while on the whole unit trusts distribute their income – although some unit trusts do provide re-investment facilities ('accumulator units'). Investment trust companies can borrow in foreign currencies to buy overseas shares, thus avoiding paying the investment currency premium, while unit trusts can raise only 'reciprocal loans' for overseas investment: these involve making an equivalent amount of sterling available in the UK to the lender.

THE MECHANICS OF INVESTMENT TRUSTS

Shares in investment trust companies are dealt in on the Stock Exchange in the same way as any other publicly quoted share. The price of the shares depends on supply and demand and is also related to the trust's net asset value, which is the net amount of the trust's assets available for distribution to the trust's shareholders. This net amount is arrived at by valuing the trust's investments and its current assets, then deducting the current liabilities plus prior charges such as fixed-interest loans. An investment trust company's shares are described as being 'at a discount' when the market price quoted is below the net asset value.

The annual management charges for most investment trusts amounts to around 0.3 per cent of the trust's total assets, but the costs of most of the larger investment trust companies are well below this level. There are no other management charges or advertising costs added to the investment trust's share price.

TYPES OF INVESTMENT TRUSTS

The orthodox investment trust is one with the longest established history, and is a trust using equity, or ordinary share capital, plus some fixed-term loans. The trusts then use the capital at their disposal to invest in UK or overseas shares – in fact one of the main attractions of most investment trust companies is that they have gone for the overseas share markets in a big way. They offer the investor the opportunity to invest in the USA, Canada, Western Europe, Japan and Australia, thus hedging his bets against the cyclical nature of the UK economy. Having built up a fund of overseas investment expertise, the managers borrow funds in foreign currency without paying the investment currency premium.

TAX AND INVESTMENT TRUSTS

Investment trust companies do offer certain taxation advantages. Corporation tax is effectively charged on the capital gains of an investment trust company at a concessionary rate equivalent to one half the basic rate of income tax. Double taxation of the investment trust company and its shareholders is prevented by giving the shareholder a tax credit at one half the basic rate of income tax on any gain he may realise on disposal. This credit reduces his own liability to capital gains tax on that gain (and the first £1,000 of gains is free of tax, while gains of up to £9,500 are liable to reduced rates of capital gains tax) and is available irrespective of the amount of gain which the investment trust company has itself realised. The effect of this tax sweetener is that no payment is required from a shareholder liable to tax on his capital gains at half the

23

basic rate of income tax. (This may well be reduced to 10 per cent as.from 1979–80.) So far as income tax is concerned the shareholder receives his dividend plus a statement of the income tax credit applicable to that dividend. The total amount of the dividend and the tax credit is set against any liability to tax on that income. A shareholder liable to income tax at the basic rate has no further tax to pay and if he is not liable to income tax, he can claim repayment from the Inland Revenue.

'SPLIT-LEVEL' TRUSTS AND OTHERS

Most of the refinements of the investment trust world have been the products of the past fifteen years. 'Split-level' investment trusts were introduced in the mid-sixties. Technically these are labelled 'split-capital' trusts and the idea of them is to give the shareholder a choice of capital gain, income, or a combination of both. Hence the names of investment trusts such as Dualvest or Triplevest, which are split-capital investment trusts. The ordinary share capital of these trusts is divided into two basic categories, income shares and capital shares (although there may also be debenture and preference shares). Unlike an 'orthodox' investment trust company, the split funds usually have a fixed life during which all or most of the income is paid to the shareholder. When the investment trust company is liquidated the income shares are repaid at a pre-arranged price and the remaining assets go to the capital shareholders.

After split-level trusts came the 'B' shares investment trusts. 'B' shareholders have equal rights with ordinary shareholders in the trusts but they normally have no rights to dividends. Instead, each receives a scrip issue with an asset value equal to the amount of the dividend paid on each ordinary share and convertible into the ordinary shares at some future date. The fact that such scrip issues are not taxable as income renders them attractive to high-rate taxpayers seeking capital growth and net income, whereas low-rate taxpayers needing high income would be attracted to the income shares of the split-level trusts.

You can also buy debenture and loan stocks issued by an

investment trust company, again attractive to low-rate tax-payers. These have final conversion dates sometime in the future, with convertibility rights into ordinary shares near the asset value at the date of issue. They offer a future interest in the equity of the investment trust company, but in the meantime carry a higher income.

Last but not least are the warrants. These are transferable certificates (in which there is a market for buying and selling) which give the holder the right to subscribe for shares in the investment company at some future date. The attraction of the warrant is that it offers an option on a future interest in the ordinary shares of the trust for a small initial investment. Warrants carry no dividend entitlement or capital gains tax credit unless the option is exercised.

THE HIDDEN DRAWBACKS

On the face of it investment trusts look most attractive to the private investor. There is the opportunity of handing over your cash to a highly trained professional manager; there are few costs; there are investment trust vehicles tailored to suit almost every need, whether for income, capital gain, or straight speculation, and there are tax sweeteners plus the opportunity of hedging your bets by investing overseas without paying the investment currency premium. But there are drawbacks. First of all the investment trusts of this country stand at a substantial discount to their net asset value. Why? The investment trust managers are perplexed and are scratching their heads for ways out of the dilemma, even to the extent of becoming 'unitised' – in other words transforming themselves into unit trusts.

The fact is that the British investing public have become less and less interested in investment trusts as they and their professional advisers have been attracted to unit trusts and insurance bonds. That has created a situation in which supply has exceeded demand for the last couple of years or more, and that over-supply has been accentuated by the fact that in 1972 forty new trusts were launched with a value of £500 million.

On the demand front, the big investment trust holders such as insurance companies have begun to lose interest, mainly because they can now find their own way into overseas investments without the trouble of going through an investment trust. Overall, of course, there has been less money going into the ordinary share market anyway and consequently an even greater loss of interest in investment trusts. So the solutions for the investment trusts are either to mop up the surplus shares on the market, a possibility which is pretty remote as it would require a change in the law to enable them to do so, or to transform themselves into the more popular unit trusts. The trouble is that this latter course of action could lead to a heavy outflow by the big investors once they had got their units in exchange for investment trust shares, so the investment trust managers do not want to start a rush for the door. The other alternative would be to boost demand by offering their attractions as an overseas investment vehicle, but since they are not allowed to advertise this option is not at present open to them.

In 1977 and 1978 the sleepy investment trust world did receive an awakening when there was a flurry of takeover bid activity. This was due to the fact that institutional fund managers such as pension fund managers woke up to the fact that they could buy large blocks of shares at less than the market price by buying an entire investment trust whose share price stood at a substantial discount to the trust's own shareholdings. Had the same pension fund been engaged in buying the same shares through the stock market, the very weight of its buying muscle would have driven up the price of the shares against it.

Chapter 4

What to Do About Rights Issues

Many a perplexed shareholder in a company making a rights issue must wonder what to do about his or her 'rights' – whether to take up the rights, sell the rights in the market 'nil paid', sell enough rights to pay for the call on the shareholders' remaining entitlement, or whether to do nothing at all. Before going on to discuss these options, we will first examine why a company has a rights issue at all, whether it is in the best interests of the shareholders, and the consequent effects on the company's share price.

WHY HAVE A RIGHTS ISSUE?

Essentially companies make rights issues to shareholders in order to raise finance with which to underpin an investment programme (money for new plant etc.) or to reduce the burden of company debt. Alternatively a company could be hard-pressed for cash and have to come to its shareholders to put up more cash because the necessary finance cannot be raised elsewhere. This latter case could be termed an 'involuntary' rights issue because the company has no alternative method open to it of raising the ready cash. The former case is basically a 'voluntary' rights issue because the company has the other options open to it of raising the necessary cash by selling equity to the investing public, or by arranging a term loan.

The flood of rights issues which took place in 1975 and 1976 was due not only to the dire straits of the capital-raising market over the preceding eighteen months, which caused many companies to get out of balance in respect of their share capital/debt ratio (with fixed debt taking too heavy a proportion of the company's capital base), but also because the transition from a corporation tax system to an imputation tax system made rights issues a more attractive capital-raising device to the company. This is due to the fact that less profit is required to service dividend payments to shareholders under the imputation system than under the corporation tax system.

WHAT ABOUT THE SHAREHOLDER?

Normally, rights issues are bad news for shareholders and tend to have been disliked by the City in the persons of the investment managers of insurance funds, investment and unit trusts and banks. A rights issue can (and most probably will) dilute the shareholder's return from the company in which he has invested because the rise in net profit on the new capital raised will usually be less than the increase in shareholders' capital.

It is first necessary to clear up a popular misconception which has probably been caused by the cosmetic effect of the name *rights* issue. There are still many investors who believe that a rights issue by the company in which they hold shares offers them the opportunity of subscribing capital on preferential terms – in other words the shareholder is getting something for nothing. What is not fully understood, or perhaps not understood at all, is that the apparent discount between the price of new shares being issued by way of rights, as against the price of the old shares, is eliminated when the shares go 'ex-rights'; the 'cum-rights' price is the market price of the shares before the rights issue.

The rights will only have a value if the market believes that the new capital being raised will earn a rate of return the same as, or greater than, the existing share capital. In order to evaluate a rights issue it is necessary for the shareholder to know to what use the capital being raised by his company's rights issue is to be put, and what sort of return will be earned from it. This would enable him, if he believes the company's projections on future earnings per share (which is the name of the game), to make a decision as to whether he should:

(a) subscribe new money;

(b) sell his rights 'nil paid';

(c) do nothing; or

(d) sell both his existing shareholding and his rights.

Having made the case for the commonsense approach to a rights issue – remember that it is rare that rights issue capital will earn the same rate of return as the shareholders' existing capital in a company, particularly if the new money is only being used to fund existing debt – it is worth looking at the actual arithmetic involved in working out the value of a 'right'.

CALCULATING THE VALUE OF A RIGHT

In calculating the value of a right to a shareholder we have to make the unlikely assumption that the rights issue capital will earn the same rate of return when employed in the shareholder's company as does the existing capital.

In a rights issue, the new shares are always issued to the existing shareholders for a price lower than the prevailing market price at the time of the issue. The formula for calculating the value of one right is to take the difference between the ex-rights price and the subscription price, and divide it by the number of rights necessary to acquire one new share. Which is saying a mouthful. The arithmetic is shown below in a worked example.

Let us suppose the Widget Manufacturing Company's shares have a prevailing market price of £2 per share. Widget's Board declares its intention to raise new capital for the greater growth of Widget Manufacturing by way of a rights issue of 10 new shares for every 10 existing shares at £1 per share.

The *cum-rights price* of a Widget's ordinary share is £2, the prevailing market price before the rights issue is made.

The *ex-rights price* will be £1.50:

	No. of shares	*Price per share*	*Total value*
Existing shareholding (say)	10	£2.00	£20.00
New shares	10	£1.00	£10.00
Total	20	—	£30.00

29

£30.00 divided by 20 = £1.50, which is therefore the ex-rights price.

The *value of one right* is calculated as follows:

Ex-rights price	£1.50
Subscription price	£1.00
Apparent gain	.50p

Normally, rights issues are bad news so far as the share-holder is concerned. The usual effect of a rights issue is to cause the company's share price to fall due to the 'dilution' effect. However, if the market is short of stock a rights issue can offer the big institutional buyer the opportunity of translating surplus cash into equity, and the share price can rise. Normally, though, rights issues are more in the interests of the company than its shareholders, and the shareholder has to be very certain about the future earnings potential of his company before taking up his rights to subscribe for new shares.

RIGHTS ISSUES: OTHER OPTIONS

The shareholder can of course sell his rights on the stock market on a 'nil paid' basis but keep his existing shareholding which has entitled him to those rights in the first place. All that nil paid means is that the shareholder pays out nothing on the rights issue but tells his stockbroker to sell the rights on the market for what they will fetch. However, such a shareholder should be aware that in a despondent market any bonus effect (ie. getting something for laying out nothing) from a rights issue can speedily be eliminated when the value of 'nil rights' can halve during a day's trading on the stock market. Selling your rights 'nil paid' depends on market conditions at the time of sale – and there is the broker's commission to come off what you might get for your 'nil paid' rights in the market place.

Another option open to the shareholder is to sell enough of his rights in the market to pay for the call on the remaining entitlement. There is rather a complex formula which calculates how many rights should be sold by the shareholder in order to render his subscription self-financing.

If the shareholder chooses to do nothing at all, then either the company's other shareholders buy his entitlement by means of an excess application form, or the shares are sold in the market and the premium, if any, is distributed to the shareholder.

The last option of all and, depending on the individual company involved, perhaps the wisest is for the shareholder to sell his existing holding along with his rights, collect any premium, and then re-invest the proceeds in an investment prospect giving a better chance of capital appreciation. This avoids the dilution effect of the rights issue.

There is usually an exception to every rule, and in the case of rights issues the exception is provided by companies which use rights issues to get round dividend limitations. An example was Croda International, which announced a rights issue which no Croda shareholder could afford to refuse. Croda offered new shares at a nominal price of 10p each against the market price of 90p and this enabled the company to double its dividend payments to shareholders in that year. The Croda rights scheme was a pathfinder at that time in that it avoided the government limitations on dividend rises as well as raising £4.4 million for the company's future growth.

Chapter 5

How to Use the Options Market

In essence, 'options' are a way of taking out an insurance policy against future fluctuations in the prices of shares. The use of options is restricted to UK shares in fact, if not in theory, because you cannot take out an option on gilt-edged stocks. Options in gilt-edged stocks were allowed once, but the use of gilt-edged options as a tax avoidance technique brought the Treasury down on this practice like a ton of bricks. Also in theory you can take out an option on overseas shares but in practice an options market in such shares is excluded by the existence of the investment currency premium which has to be paid when buying overseas shares.

THE MECHANICS OF THE OPTIONS MARKET

There are plenty of experienced investors who have never used the options market in their lives. An option is just what the name implies. Instead of buying a chunk of shares direct, the options market exists so that you can buy a three-month option over the same chunk of shares but for a much smaller outlay. Let's say you are interested in buying 5,000 shares in a particular company, and the shares stand at £1 each in the market. Instead of laying out £5,000 you could buy an option over the same 5,000 shares for around 10 per cent of their market value, so you would only lay out £500 instead of £5,000 (plus dealing expenses, of course). If you had decided to buy the 5,000 shares for £5,000 direct, and if the shares double within three months, the £5,000 invested in your 5,000 shares is now worth £10,000 so you have made a very handsome £5,000 profit before capital gains tax.

But suppose that, instead of shelling out £5,000 to buy the shares, you had only spent £500 to buy an option over the same amount of shares. The 5,000 shares double in price to £10,000. The cost of exercising your option (at the option price of £1 per share, the market price prevailing at the time you took out your option) is £5,000. If you then sell the shares in the market at their new £2 price you pick up a capital gain of £5,000 which, less your option money of £500, gives you a windfall profit of £4,500 before capital gains tax. Now to get this windfall you have only had to lay out £500 – you have been able to 'gear up' by using the options market. This device leaves your true speculator with most of his capital intact to pursue other, possibly more lucrative opportunities, instead of tying it all up in one block of shares.

Of course every silver lining has a cloud attached to it, as many a speculator has found out. The disadvantage of the options technique used to be that if the shares on which you bought an option went down in price so far that the option was not worth exercising, then you lost all your option money, so you just had a dead loss on your hands. Since April 1978 you can trade call options on certain shares on the Stock Exchange before maturity, so you can get out before an option's maturity date is reached instead of taking a dead loss.

ARRANGING AN OPTION PURCHASE

The options facility has been part and parcel of the London investment scene for well over a century. How do you go about arranging an option? You can do so through your own stock-broker or through your clearing bank's stockbroker if you do not have a direct relationship with a stockbroker. He then gets onto one of the option dealers whose job it is in life to perform a 'jobbing' function in the options corner of the stock market.

Normally brokers talk about three-months options, but in fact the option period varies between two and a half and three months. As each new Stock Exchange account day opens, the option period is three months – and the option period then dwindles down to two and a half months until the arrival of the next account day restores the period of the option to three months. By the way, remember that an option holder is deemed to have abandoned his option unless it is exercised on the last declaration date, which is shown on the original contract note. Normally this is a Thursday, twelve days before a Stock Exchange account day.

In stock market parlance, a 'bull' in the options market is someone who exercises his option (and remember that if you do exercise your option you get, as an added sweetener, any dividends which have accrued to the shares over which you hold the option during the period of the option). A 'bear' is the chap who fails to exercise his option and kisses his option money goodbye, or trades his option before maturity for cash.

'CALL OPTIONS'

The options market may seem complex, but the principle is simple enough. Where some investors get discouraged is when they hear talk of 'call options', 'put options', 'put and call options' and 'taking option money', but there is nothing complex about this sort of jargon.

A 'call option' is the commonest type of option, giving the buyer the right to buy a block of shares three months into the future at today's share price. In fact, you do have to pay slightly over the odds because you have to pay a few pence more than the shares' current market price in order to remunerate the option broker for his work in making sure he can deliver those shares to you when you exercise your option three months hence. The amount of this premium is small – only 1p-2p for example on an ICI share. And here we come to another way of regarding the options market: some investors use the market for insurance rather than speculative purposes, to protect an existing capital gain. Let's suppose you had the good fortune to buy 10,000 ICI shares at £1.18 a share back in January 1975 when ICI shares were yielding 14.6 per cent and the *Financial Times* 30-Share Index stood at 146.6. A couple of years later you would have become the complacent owner of 8,474 ICI shares worth £3.60 each; total £30,506. So you would have been sitting on a capital profit to the tune of £18,700. With all the economic and political uncertainties about at that time, you would have wanted to protect this capital gain, and who would have blamed you? You could have used the options market by selling your shares (a capital gain is not a gain until you actually sell and collect the cash) and re-investing a small proportion of the profit by buying a call option on the same number of ICI shares. So, for this comparatively small outlay you would have bought the certainty of being able to get your shareholding back if the price had kept on rising, plus the certainty that, if the ICI share price had nose-dived you would have got your capital gain safely tucked away. The only drawback to this technique is that by selling you do attract capital gains tax, but capital gains tax is going to have to be paid on your gain (if you still have a gain) some time unless the shares are held into perpetuity, or the share price falls and your gain becomes a loss, or capital gains tax is abolished.

'PUT OPTIONS'

A put option is an option to sell a block of shares in three months time at the market price prevailing for the shares at the time you take out your put option. So if the share price falls you make a profit, while if it rises you let your option lapse. It is merely an extension of the bear share operation principle: selling shares you do not have in the belief that the price will fall and you will be able to buy back at the lower price to settle the transaction by the next account date. You can also use a put option for insurance purposes because for a modest outlay you can ensure the sale of your shareholding at a known price. For example, you can use a put option to ensure that you can sell shares for the current market price in three months time, even if the share price falls back during that time.

'PUT OR CALL OPTIONS'

A put or call option is a double option. This technique means that you can exercise either a call option or a put option (but not both) three months in the future. As you would expect, a double option costs nearly double the price. Using double options can be a useful investment technique when the stock market is very volatile, which has become the norm over the past few years. If you do not know which way the market will move next but you think it could rise or fall by a substantial amount, then a double option gives you the opportunity to make money out of an upward or downward movement. As with a call or put option, the price of the share must move by more than the cost of the option, to make a double option worth exercising.

'TAKING OPTION MONEY'

Taking option money is something which not many investors know about. Let's suppose you have £30,000 worth of shares in different companies. You can tell your stockbroker that you are willing to sell an option on any or all of them. Your broker then advises an option dealer, and if he hears of an opportunity he will get in touch with your broker who will then tell you what the terms of the offer are. Let's suppose you have a block of shares worth £3.00 apiece and you tell your broker that you would like to be offered option money of 30p a share with an option exercise price of £3.03. If the shares go up, then the option will be exercised and you will sell your shares for £3.03 per share plus the 30p option money (less the option dealer's cut and your broker's commission). If the price of your share falls and the option is not exercised then you keep your shares, but you get the option money (less expenses) of 30p a share for your pains.

OPTIONS AND CAPITAL GAINS TAX

What about capital gains tax? If you buy an option and do not exercise it then your lost option money is not allowable as a capital loss. If you exercise your option then it is part and parcel of the overall deal – in fact it can be worth exercising your option just to get a capital loss if you have a gain against which to offset it. What it boils down to is that if you have laid out £200 in option money and the share over which you have an option goes down, it can still be worth exercising the option and incurring an additional loss of say £50–£60, because this gives you an allowable capital loss of £250–£260 as against a dead loss of £200. But you need that capital gain against which to offset it.

TRADING IN OPTIONS

The problem with the 'traditional' options market was that it was somewhat inflexible – either the investor exercised his option on maturity or let it lapse and accepted a dead loss. The London options trading market was introduced in April 1978 to provide more flexibility because it is now possible, on a number of 'blue chip' shares, to buy and sell 'call options' during their life (ie. before maturity). Before getting into the intricacies of the market, let's spell out just who the market is designed for so you can relate it to your own position.

The Relevance of the Traded Options Market

The private investor can use the traded options market either as an insurance market, if he is a conservative investor, or as a gambler's market – using the 'gearing up facility' – if he likes high-risk speculation.

The Insurance Element

Going back to our traditional options market, we explained how the investor could take option money to protect himself against a fall in the Stock Market. In exactly the same way, the private investor with a substantial portfolio can write call options against the shares he holds. He then picks up the premium paid by the investor who buys the option from him. If the share price rises, the investor writing the call option loses out. If it falls he has protected himself by the amount of the premium earned. It is a means of getting an extra return from your share portfolio, if you are a reasonably big investor.

Alternatively, suppose you reckon that the Stock Market is going to continue trading within a narrow range. If interest rates offer a good rate of return you could put most of your capital into high-yielding gilts, into a Building Society, or on the money market. You could keep back, say, 5 per cent of your capital to buy call options – in a number of blue chip shares – and so insure yourself against any sudden upward movement in the Stock Market which you had not anticipated.

If the Stock Market does not take off, you can sell your call options in the traded options market and recoup some of the money you have invested. In addition you have the comfort of knowing that the majority of your capital has been earning high interest elsewhere.

Another situation in which you can use the traded options market is one where you suspect a company share price may move sharply upwards – perhaps because of a takeover bid or because of an (as yet) undeclared discovery, such as a North Sea Oil find. If you prove correct in your guesstimate, then you reap the reward. If you prove wrong then you have limited the amount of your loss to a comparatively small amount.

You can also use the traded options market to reduce risk. Let's suppose you feel the whole Stock Market, or a particular share or share sector, is going to nosedive. You could sell your portfolio of shares, or that particular share, and reckon on buying them (it) later at a lower price. If you are wrong, then you have lost out – quite heavily if you sell off the whole of your portfolio. But you can use the traded options market to provide you with insurance against being wrong. You can sell your shares, but at the same time, you can buy traded call options against them. If the market falls, you are only liable to lose – at worst – your option money. If the market proves you wrong, then you can exercise your options and re-invest at a predetermined price in the stocks which you sold earlier.

These are all the insurance arguments for the traded options market. The practical difficulty is presented by the fact that only a small number of shares offer a traded options facility. When the market first opened these were: British Petroleum, Commercial Union, Consolidated Goldfields, Courtaulds, GEC, Grand Metropolitan, ICI, Land Securities, Marks & Spencer and Shell. The comparatively small number of shares with UK traded options compares with the 200 US stocks in which it is possible to use traded options on the Chicago Board Options Exchange. By the way, there are similar markets in traded options in Toronto, Montreal, Sydney, Singapore and Amsterdam. It is hoped to add to the UK list gradually – gradually because the UK Stock Exchange is hoping to avoid the stream of abuses reported by the US Securities and Exchange Commission which ended in the latter placing a moratorium on any further expansion of options business.

The Speculator

In addition to the insurance arguments, there are also the attractions of the traded options market to the speculator – to the chap who is prepared to take high risks to secure commensurately high rewards. The first technique the speculator can use is to buy traded options in order to increase his gearing, a point briefly touched on at the outset. As is the case in the traditional options market, the premium paid for a traded call option is only a small percentage of the cost of the share. The speculator can therefore take an interest in many more shares by using options than by buying the related shares outright. Hence the term 'gearing' or 'leverage', both of which mean putting a limited amount of money to the maximum use.

Before we go on to show how the technique can be used, we need to explain a little traded options jargon.

Class of Options: All call options relating to the same underlying share form a single class.

Series of Options: All options of the same class which have the same exercise price and expiry date, and which relate to the same number of shares, form a single series.

Expiry Dates: When trading in an option is established there is a choice of three 'expiry dates' – three, six and nine months ahead. For example, the full picture of, say, Land Securities options could be as follows:

Share price	Exercise price	Latest prices of traded options		
		July	*October*	*January*
208p	180p	31p	33p	37p
	200p	14½p	19½p	25p
	220p	5p	11p	15½p

As you can see, there is a choice of three expiry dates ahead – in July, October and January. Hence you have Land Securities July Series, October Series and January Series. There are series for each expiry date with 'exercise prices' of 180p, 200p and 220p. When the July option expires a new 9-month series, finishing in the next April, will be opened for trading.

The price (or premium) of the option in each series fluctuates according to supply and demand in the market, and this is governed by the price of the underlying share, the striking price of the option and the length of its life. The three exercise prices of Land Securities in the example above are 180p, 200p and 220p, and the shares stand at 208p in the Stock Market. The price for the 'July 180's' is 31p and for the 'July 200's' it is 14½p, while for the 'July 220's' it is only 5p. As you can readily appreciate, while the Land Securities' share price stands at 208p in the market, the 'July 180's' are worth at least 28p (208p−180p=28p) against the traded option price of 31p. However, the 'July 220's' are without intrinsic value because the exercise price is greater than the share price (220p as against 208p).

The reason why the traded options prices increase – with the Land Securities July 180's at 31p as against the January price of 37p, or the 220's at 5p as against 15½p is because an option with a life of 6 or 9 months is obviously more valuable than one with a life of only three months, because there is greater opportunity for the underlying share to grow in value over a longer period.

An option which has an exercise price below that of the underlying share price is said to be *in the money*. An option with an exercise price which is higher than the share price is described as being *out of the money*. For example, the buyer of the Land Securities January 220's is paying 15½p in the above example, knowing that the share price stands at only 208p as against 220p, which is his exercise price in January. He has to hope that before the expiry date the Land Securities share price will rise above 220p. If it does not then the option will ultimately be worthless.

The *unit of trading* in the traded options market describes the number of shares to which a single option contract relates. This is normally 1,000 shares, so if you want to trade in the options on 5,000 shares you place an order for *5 contracts* and *not for 5,000 options*.

Returning to the possibilities the market opens up to the dyed-in-the-wool speculator, let us suppose that the shares of Company A stand at £4 or 400p. There are three series of traded options – the July 380's which are at a 40p premium (or price), the July 410's which are at 15p and the July 440's which are at 5p.

Leaving aside dealing expenses (we will come to these later) the speculator could buy 500 shares for £2,000, or 2 July 380 Contracts for £800, (2 contracts) or 5 July 410 Contracts for £750 (or 5 contracts), or 10 July 440 Contracts at 5p (or 10 Contracts). If he buys the shares direct then he gains, or loses, as the share price moves and he remains the owner of the shares until he decides to sell them. But let's look at the speculator's position as against the movement in the underlying share price shown below.

Outright Purchase	Cost	Share Price at Expiry Date of Options					
		380p	400p	420p	440p	460p	480p
500 shares@400p	£2000	−£100	Even	+£100	+£200	+£300	+£400
or:							
2 Jul 380 Contracts@40p	£800	−£800	−£400	Even	+£400	+£800	+£1,200
5 Jul 410 Contracts@15p	£750	−£750	−£750	−£250	+£750	+£1,750	+£2,750
10 Jul 440 Contracts@5p	£500	−£500	−£500	−£500	−£500	+£1,500	+£3,500

Let us look at these figures more carefully, because if you understand them you will catch the point of both traded options and gearing, and with it a whiff of the excitement of true speculation. Take the case of outright purchase of 500 shares at £4 apiece. The share price has to move up to 400p before the investor breaks even (and we are not allowing for dealing costs) and even if it rises to 480p the investor only makes a profit of £400.

If we take the next case, the chap who buys two contracts (or 2,000 shares) at an exercise price of 380p and at a cost of 40p then this costs him immediately £800. When the share price moves up to 420p, he breaks even because at that price he can exercise his option over 2,000 shares at 380p=£7,600 for a total cost, including his option money, of £7,600+ £800=£8,400, and can sell his 2,000 shares at 420p=£8,400. By the time the share moves up to 480p then he is in profit to the tune of £1,200. (Costs=£8,400 while 2,000 shares@480p can be sold for £9,600 giving him a £1,200 profit.) And he makes that profit on an outlay of only £800 as against the £2,000 laid out by the chap who buys the shares outright. In the third case, the speculator buys 5 contracts (5,000 shares) at an exercise price of 410p for a premium of 15p, costing him £750. Until the underlying share price moves up to 440p he is losing money – but at 440p he jumps into sizeable profits showing how the gearing works. At his exercise price of 410p he can exercise his option over 5,000 shares for £20,500, to which he adds his option money of £750 making an overall total of £21,250. But he can sell those 5,000 shares at 440p per share – or £22,000 and so makes a profit of £750. When the share price moves up to 480p his profits increase to £2,750 on an outlay of £750.

The speculator who pays the least – only 5p option money – buys 10 contracts, or 10,000 shares for an outlay of only £500, with an exercise price of 440p. He does not move into a profit situation until the share price reaches 460p but the turn round from a loss of £500 to a profit of £1,500 is dramatic as the share moves up to the 460p level. At his exercise price of 440p he takes up 10,000 shares on which he has an option and this costs him £44,000 plus his option money of £500, making £44,500 in all. But his 10,000 shares can be sold for £46,000 and this produces a £1,500 profit. At the 480p level his profit increases to £3,500 for an outlay of £500. Throughout the transaction his maximum possible loss remained at £500, and the facility of a 'secondary' traded options market means that he could have limited that loss by selling his option before maturity if he had felt like doing so.

There are (inevitably) a number of pitfalls. One is that there is no dividend entitlement on traded options, unlike traditional options. Second, there is the vexed question of tax. Traded options are not treated for tax in a similar way to shares, where the liability is to capital gains tax if you make a profit. Traded options are treated by the Revenue as 'wasting assets', which results in an anomalous situation under which the investor can make a loss, but still have to pay tax on a theoretic gain. For example, suppose you pay 50p for a traded option in the ICI October 330's series, if you sell this option half way through its life for 60p you will not make a 10p profit in the eyes of the Revenue. They will reckon that you have made a gain of 30p because the option is half way through its life and therefore will value the option on that basis. On the same ridiculous basis you can make a 10p loss but the Revenue will insist that you made a 15p profit. It is much the same nonsensical situation that the Revenue used to apply to the warrants market, and there are moves afoot to stop it and have it replaced by the normal Capital Gains Tax system.

Another pitfall to options trading is that the rules require you to settle the next morning. There is no 'in and out' during the Account without using any capital in the process. The traded options market insists that you pay up, in full, the next morning. The Stock Exchange are so keen to ensure that the market is run properly that every broker involved must give a client who wants to take part in the traded options market a stiff Letter of Agreement which has to be signed by the client, showing that he has read and understood it and will abide by it.

Talking of brokers brings us to the question of dealing costs. As a general rule of thumb guide, you need to see (tax considerations apart) a 10 per cent to 15 per cent gain in your traded option before you break even and move into profit in order to pay for your dealing expenses. But, looking on the bright side, in a steeply rising market (which happened to coincide with the launch of the London traded options market) gains in options can be much greater than 10 per cent or 15 per cent.

The last piece of the traded options jigsaw puzzle is *'uncovered'* or *'naked' writing*, and we are not being pornographic. So far we have assumed that the chap who writes the option (akin to taking option money in the traditional options market) actually has the shares concerned. However, you can write an option which is not covered by the ownership of the shares in question – hence 'uncovered' or 'naked' writing. But the naked writer does have to put up a cash margin at the traded options Clearing House (or provide a guarantee) to the value of at least 25 per cent of the day-to-day value of the underlying share, adjusted by the amount by which the option series is in or out of the money. This is the highest risk strategy to pursue because there is no limit to the losses which can be made; the writer has an obligation to deliver at a fixed price the shares relating to the options, and the price of these may have doubled (perhaps as a result of a takeover bid) since the option was written. However, if the naked writer keeps his position open and the share price is below the exercise price of the option at the date of expiry, then he gets the entire amount of the premium, so it is a case of high risk/high reward.

The London traded options market got off to a pretty slow start initially, with a few shares having traded options and not enough writers of options about. This was because the institutional shareholders were not interested in writing options due to the small size of the market. This, in turn, has led to the traded options market makers writing options on their own account, and this produced an unwelcome volatility in option prices as such traders rush to close their positions in what soon becomes a self-feeding movement. But the market could continue to grow.

Chapter 6

Warrants – a Gambler's Market

In the Square Mile of the City of London, the pundits will tell you that warrants are for experts only, and that the spectacular increases and precipitous falls in warrant prices, allied with the lack of understanding as to just what the warrant market is all about, render investment in warrants a hazardous business for the amateur. There certainly is some truth in the argument that warrants experience price fluctuations which are much more volatile than ordinary shares. For example, if you had had the good fortune to buy shares in the dog days of January 1975 then you would have had to be unlucky not to double your money within three months by investing in any representative selection of blue-chip shares. However, had you invested in, say, Cavenham warrants at the same time your capital would have produced more than a 500 per cent increase over the same period. There is certainly a lack of understanding about the warrants market, and the experts in it swathe their manipulations with all the mystical mumbo jumbo of 'gearing effects', 'conversion premiums' and 'volatility factors', which can cause the amateur to retreat in dismay.

WHAT ARE WARRANTS?

Warrants present only capital gain opportunities and pay the holder no income. Therein lies their secret. Surtax payers, for obvious reasons, are not interested in income but they are interested in capital gain because the latter attracts a much lower rate of tax. Warrants, which really had their heyday back in the bull market of 1972, are pieces of paper, issued by

45

a company or by an investment trust, which give the buyer an option to buy a pre-determined number of the company's ordinary shares at a pre-determined price during a pre-determined period of time in the future. In theory at least the warrant provides three additional benefits to the buyer. One is that, instead of locking up money in a slab of a company's ordinary shares, the investor can buy warrants giving him rights to buy the same number of shares at a known price sometime in the future for, normally, a fraction of the cost. This means that he releases his capital to pursue other investment opportunities. Let us take for our example a share, perhaps in an investment trust, which has a market price of 51p. A holding of 10,000 shares would cost the shareholder (exclusive of dealing expenses etc.) £5,100. However, the investor has the alternative of buying the same investment trust's warrants for 19p, which gives him the right of converting into the same shares, on the basis of one share per warrant, at a price of £1 until, say, 1990. This means that rights over the same 10,000 shares will 'only' cost him £1,900, thus releasing £3,200 for investment elsewhere. And in the heyday of speculation, when punters borrowed cash with which to finance their stock market operations, the warrant technique lowered their interest costs while maximising their capital gain opportunities.

A second benefit provided by warrants is that of liquidity. Buying warrants does not mean that you have to lock up cash for a period of years. The existence of an active market in which you can buy and sell warrants means that you can turn them into cash if need be.

A third benefit is that, despite the fact that warrants can produce much greater capital gains opportunities when the stock market is recovering from a really vicious bear market, the price of warrants does not fall, in the same downward spiral as shareholders panic to sell, as far as the price of the related ordinary share. The reason for this is that the warrant price, being normally a fraction of the price of the related ordinary share, sooner or later falls to a point beyond which it can fall no further. It joins the ranks of the 'penny stocks', and even though the price of the ordinary share still has some way to fall, the price of the warrant cannot become a negative amount so long as the company which has issued it stays solvent. So when the market turns, the warrants can chalk up really spectacular gains in the initial buying rush as the professionals scent the opportunity to make a massive capital gain by buying warrants giving them rights to shares at a set price.

THE 'GEARING EFFECT'

The opportunities for big capital gains are provided (and here we come to our first bit of jargon) by the 'gearing effect'. The price of warrants moves in the same direction as the price of the shares to which they are linked. However, in percentage terms, the price of warrants moves up faster in a bull market, and goes down faster in a bear market, before stopping at the 'penny stock' floor. To take a practical example of the gearing effect at work, suppose a share worth £1 in the market has related warrants entitling the holder to buy shares in the company at £1 at the end of five years, and these warrants are quoted in the market at 35p. If the ordinary share price rises to £1.10 (an increase of 10 per cent), the effect of this rise could be to push up the value of the warrants to 40p (an increase of 14.3 per cent). Thus the warrant price would have gone up faster than the share price, but the same would be true in reverse in a downward movement; the fall would be correspondingly steeper.

WHY DO WARRANTS EXIST?

Investment trusts have been prolific issuers of warrants, principally for technical reasons. Back in the heady bull market days of 1972 investment trusts had something of a marketing problem. In an investment trust 'offer for sale' it was difficult to persuade investors to buy shares in the investment trust at the offer price – 'at par' – because investment trust shares then (and still today) stood at a hefty discount to their net asset value. Warrants were therefore issued to overcome this problem, and were offered as a particular sweetener to the surtax-paying investor. The majority of warrants available on today's stock market are left over from the bull market of

1972. In the company sector, the companies involved are either in property, or the ex-'go-go' stocks of 1972. A number of companies, such as Jessel Securities, have been left by the wayside during the years that witnessed the most dramatic financial traumas since the 1930s.

WARRANTS – TIPS TO REMEMBER

The main point to bear firmly in mind about warrants is that the price at which a warrant is bought and sold on the stock market is entirely separate from the subscription price, which is the pre-determined price at which the warrant can be converted into a company's ordinary shares at a pre-determined date in the future.

Going back to our example of the hypothetical investment trust warrant, this entitles the holder to one share on the final exercise date which is in 1990, at a subscription price of £1 per share. The investment trust warrant can be bought and sold in today's market for 19p. The investment trust ordinary share can be bought and sold in today's market at 51p.

The 'conversion premium' which the experts talk about is simply the premium you pay for buying warrants against buying the same company's ordinary shares. The following example shows you how to work out the conversion premium. Let us suppose a company has shares currently quoted at 40p per 10p ordinary share. The warrants issued by the company are quoted at 12p. The warrants give the holder the right to subscribe for one share in the company at £1.35 any time between 1979 and 1983. The arithemetic for working out the conversion premium is as follows:

Warrant market price	12p
Warrant conversion price	135p
	147p
Less: market value of company's ordinary share	40p
	107p

The conversion premium $= \dfrac{107p}{40p} = 267\%$

As you can readily see from the above example, the conversion premium is the theoretical extra price (over and above what you can buy the company's ordinary shares for) which the investor pays when he buys a warrant at its quoted price – *assuming he will hold it to maturity and then exercise his conversion rights* (at 135 pence per share in the above example).

The 'volatility factor' bandied about by the warrant market experts just means price fluctuations with another pseudo-scientific name. It is supposed to provide some indication of how speculative the warrants are in the light of the frequency of the price movements (volatility) of the underlying share to which the warrant is linked. The more volatile the share price, the more attractive are the warrants, because they present the holder with more frequent opportunities to buy and sell and so increase the rate of his capital gains opportunities (or, it should be stressed, the rate of his capital losses).

The best way to evaluate warrants is not to attach too much importance to gearing ratios and volatility factors but to use your commonsense and always bear in mind that warrants are a gambler's market. Warrants, like racehorses, fundamentally have a set of odds attached to them. The high risk-reward ratio could be assessed just as well by a bookmaker as by a warrant expert at 16–7 against or 5–4 on, if he took the trouble to discover just what ingredients make up 'the form'.

The three golden rules to remember are:

(a) the warrant market is a gambler's market;
(b) ask yourself if the warrant you are buying gives you a good deal in commonsense terms; and
(c) work out the likely effect on the warrant price of the movement in the underlying share price.

Chapter 7

Convertibles – the Two-Way Investment

'Convertibles' are not popular among the investing public as an alternative to investing in ordinary shares direct or by way of unit or investment trusts, in gilt-edged stock or by placing their money on deposit with banks, local authorities or with building societies. The main reason is that many private investors are not sure just what sort of animal a convertible stock is and how to evaluate it.

A convertible is an investment which occupies a sector somewhere between fixed-interest stocks and equities. By buying a convertible, the investor gets a fixed annual income which is determined by the market price he has paid for the convertible, and by its 'nominal' rate of interest. For example, a buyer of a convertible having an interest rate of 9½ per cent for each £100 nominal worth of stock, and paying a market price of £70 for the latter can work out his annual income as follows:

$$\frac{9\frac{1}{2}\% \times £100 \text{ nominal}}{£70 \text{ market price}} = 13.57\% \text{ (a yield of £13.57 for every £100 invested).}$$

In addition, the investor gains a further option which is not available to the buyer of the 'straight' fixed-interest stock. He buys the opportunity to convert his loan stock into the particular company's ordinary shares at a known price during a predetermined future period.

It is essential to bear in mind from the outset that the movements in the market price of a convertible loan stock closely follow the price of the company's shares.

50

TYPES OF CONVERTIBLE LOAN STOCKS

There are a number of varieties of convertible loan stocks which are quoted on the Stock Exchange. The bulk of convertibles being bought and sold are of the 'straight' variety. These account for around four-fifths of the market in terms of nominal (as opposed to market) value. Next in order of importance are the 'partly convertible' loan stocks which account for about one-tenth of the market. These give the buyer the right to convert part of his investment into the ordinary shares of the company at some future date. 'Subscription' stocks give the buyer an income plus the right to subscribe cash for shares in a company at a future date. 'Warrants' provide the buyer with no income, but do provide the right to subscribe cash for shares at a future date – and are of obvious interest to high tax payers. Then there are the sterling/dollar (and sterling/other 'hard' currencies) convertibles which provide a fixed income payable in sterling plus the option to convert into US or other overseas equities at a future date.

THE ADVANTAGES OF CONVERTIBLES TO THE INVESTOR

By buying a convertible, the investor is buying an insurance 'cushion'. If the investor buys shares in a company, the price of the shares can be subject to very volatile movements. A convertible does not fall so far (in terms of its market price) in a bear market as does the price of the related share. The other side of the picture, of course, is that the price of a convertible does not move up as high as the price of the ordinary share during a bull market. But the 'cushion' effect of convertibles comes into its own in a really vicious bear market such as 1974 when the market price of the convertible reaches a 'floor' when its yield becomes equal to that of fixed-interest securities which have no conversion rights.

Another advantage of convertibles is that the income they provide is normally higher than that provided by way of dividend from the company's ordinary shares, and there is the additional sweetener that this income is safer than ordinary share dividends. In fact, both income and capital invested in

51

and arising from convertible loan stocks are safer than ordinary shares because convertibles rank for payment in front of shares in the event of a liquidation. This being said, it is worth uttering a word of caution. Convertibles are normally issued by companies on an unsecured basis for the very good reason that this relieves the company from reducing the amount of chargeable assets available for further borrowing. So if a company goes to the wall, while the convertible stock holder gets preferential treatment to the ordinary shareholder, he is still part and parcel of the unsecured creditors so far as the liquidator is concerned.

What other advantages are there for the investor in convertibles? In addition to the guaranteed capital appreciation (as long as the stock is bought for less than its nominal value) before the exercise of the conversion rights, there are potential rewards accruing from participation, even after the conversion rights are exercised, in a growth-oriented company. In the longer term, cool analysis may provide the answer that the risk to the private investor in buying convertible loan stocks issued by growth-oriented companies may be less than the risk to him provided by the erosive effects of inflation if he is keeping his capital in cash on deposit over the same period. In fact, when the clouds of economic gloom settle menacingly on the investment horizon, the convertible, particularly the short-dated convertible standing at below its nominal value, becomes an attractive 'hedge' investment.

WHO ISSUES CONVERTIBLES AND WHY

To the company issuing the convertibles, the stock provides an opportunity to raise capital – possibly to be used to finance an acquisition – for which the rate of interest will be lower than that for a straight (non-convertible) loan. This device also avoids the necessity of watering down the company's own equity base, which would happen if more ordinary shares were issued. The effect of the future conversion rights on the convertible loan stock is to create deferred ordinary shares at a higher price level than the prevailing market price at the times of issue, whereas ordinary shares issues are normally made at a discount to the prevailing market price.

Who issues convertibles? Most stem from the financial sector – banks, property companies (which account for around one-fifth of the convertibles issued) and investment trusts. During the bear market of 1974–5 a number of companies and investment trusts were to the forefront in 'buying back' their own convertible loan stocks. For example, investment trusts can reduce the prospective dilution in their own shares (after the conversion rights are exercised) by buying back their convertible loan stock. A cash-rich manufacturing company can also avoid this dilution by buying back when it believes that its convertible loan stock is oversold due to adverse market sentiment, and that the yield it provides has reached an abnormal level.

Other points of interest about convertibles are that well over half of all convertibles issued are for amounts of under £5 million, but account for only one-fifth of the market. Approaching 20 per cent of convertibles are for amounts of over £10 million, but account for well over half the market in terms of nominal value.

THE PREMIUM – TWO EXAMPLES

The biggest pitfall for the investor to grasp if he wants to buy convertible loan stocks is how to evaluate the 'premium', which will tell him whether the convertible in question is 'cheap' or 'dear'.

The premium is the difference between the market price of a company's ordinary shares and the effective conversion price into that company's ordinary shares of the related convertible loan stock. The premium is the price you pay for the extra safety provided by the convertible – and as a general yardstick, in normal market conditions, if the premium is more than three times the difference between the convertible's yield and the yield offered by the related ordinary share, then the convertible is a 'dear buy'.

How do you work out the premium? Below is a worked example. Bear in mind at the outset that the extra cost, or premium, of an investment in a convertible loan stock is expressed as a percentage of the cost of the equity in the convertible loan stock.

Let us suppose that the price of this stock is £56 per £100 nominal. The conversion terms are 200 shares in XYZ Company for every £100 nominal of stock held – giving a 'nominal' conversion price of 50p as against, let us say, the market price of 15p per XYZ ordinary share.

This means that the investor buying XYZ convertible loan stock at a price of £56 buys conversion rights into 200 shares in XYZ – an effective market price of 28p. He is paying a premium for the conversion rights of 28p minus 15p (the effective conversion price of the convertible loan stock less the current market price of the XYZ ordinary shares) which is 13p. The difference of 13p compared with a market price of 15p throws up a premium of 13/15=86.7 per cent.

So the XYZ Company convertible loan stock is still a dear buy, even though it is offering a very high running yield of 16.7 per cent. The lesson to be learned is: do not evaluate a convertible loan stock just by the income it offers you. Work out the premium to establish whether you are paying over the odds. The premium can be very small, or even negative.

CONVERSION TIMING

Reverting from the particular to the general, at what time should you convert your convertible loan stock? For convertible loan stocks having long option conversion periods, the best time to convert is normally towards the end of the conversion period. However, if the dividends from the relative shares overtake the fixed interest income from the convertible during the option conversion period, then holders should convert. Generally speaking there is no incentive to convert until the last opportunity unless income is lost. The premium should also be watched carefully: as a rule, the higher the premium is, the less incentive is there to convert into the company's ordinary shares. The convertible can then either be retained and regarded as a fixed interest investment or can be sold.

Chapter 8

Successful Investment in Overseas Stock Markets

The private investor who is interested in the stock market tends to think only of share dealing within the UK. Yet the lesson of the 1970s has been that, while world stock markets tend to move together as interrelated world economies sink back into recession or burst into a growth period, the astute investor should keep one eye warily open for what is happening in the main overseas stock markets. Overseas stock markets can outperform the UK stock market and even, when the UK stock market is falling, a particular overseas stock market can be chalking up a gain.

Table 4. *Performance in the Five Main Stock Markets 1970–6*

	% 1970	% 1971	% 1972	% 1973	% 1974	% 1975	% 1976
USA	−2.5	+12.3	+14.3	−19.6	−30.9	+30.5	+18.7
Japan	−15.6	+48.6	+121.2	−21.8	−17.8	+16.8	+21.9
Germany	−26.7	+19.6	+14.6	−8.0	+11.9	+25.0	+3.9
France	−8.7	−2.7	+20.0	−0.2	−27.1	+36.8	−26.3
UK	−9.8	+42.6	+0.6	−28.9	−54.3	+103.5	−17.9

(The index used to measure the five main markets is that of Capital International which has been adjusted in the light of exchange rate fluctuations relative to the US dollar)

Table 4 shows the performance of the four main stock markets overseas – the USA, Japan, Germany, France – and

Table 5. *Performance in the Five Main Stock Markets in 1977*

	Market change over 1977 (%)	*. Index used*
USA	−0.5	New York Stock Exchange
Japan	−2.6	Nikkei-Dow
Germany	+7.0	Commerzbank
France	−6.5	CAC Index
UK	+42.0	*Financial Times* 30-Share Index

their comparison with the UK. As you can readily see, if you had been fully invested in UK shares in 1971, you would have picked up a useful 42 per cent capital gain. But if you had been fully invested in Japan, your gain would have been nearer 50 per cent. If you had invested in UK shares in 1972 you would have registered a minuscule 0.6 per cent capital appreciation, but if you had invested in the Tokyo stock exchange, the capital value of your share portfolio would have chalked up a massive 121 per cent jump. In fact you could have done better during the three years 1970 to 1973 if you had invested in the highly volatile Hong Kong stock market, which recorded gains of 36 per cent in 1970, 70 per cent in 1971 and 143 per cent in 1972, thereby providing the world's best stock market performance in the three years. In the gloom and despondency days of 1974, when the *Financial Times* 30-share index went plummeting towards 150 during the three-day week caused by the miners' strike, you would have lost half the value of your shares during the year if you were a UK shareholder. Yet, in the same year, if you had managed to switch into German shares you would have actually recorded a gain of just on 12 per cent.

Despite the predictions of the experts at the beginning of 1977, you would have done badly if you had invested in the US or Japanese stock markets, which recorded losses despite the strengths of their respective economies compared with that of the British. In defiance of logic (and logic is one good way to lose money if you are a share punter interested in following it) the UK stock market dumbfounded the experts by showing a 42 per cent capital gain.

The lesson of all these facts and figures is the same as the lesson of chapter 1 – shares are for dealing in. The perfect investor (who does not exist) makes money by getting into shares at the bottom of each bear market and out of them at the top of each bull market. That is within the confines of the UK stock market, of course. The pluperfect investor would not only manage to do this, but he would also switch his portfolio into different stock markets so that he could achieve the highest possible capital gain by selecting the best stock market (among the markets in which it is possible to deal with reasonable facility) for a particular period.

Such a perfect investor (it is wonderful what the benefit of hindsight will do for a portfolio) would have taken £100 at the beginning of 1971 and invested it in Japanese equities. By shrewdly continuing in the Japanese market in 1972, and then switching into the French stock market in 1973 (assuming he wanted to stay fully invested in ordinary shares, whatever their nationality) he would have built up his capital to £326. Had he then switched his capital across the border into Germany in 1974 (a year in which the UK market nose-dived), followed by an astute transfer into the UK in 1975 and then back into the Japanese market in 1976 he would have ended up worth £906. And had he stayed in UK equities in 1977 he would have translated his £100 worth of capital into between £1,200 and £1,300.

THE INVESTMENT CURRENCY PREMIUM

Such percipience is held by few, if any. For one thing it is not an easy matter for the UK private investor to follow the movements in main share prices in the UK stock market. Following the movements of individual companies, industrial sectors and economies in the US, Japan, France and Germany compounds the problem. For another, the private investor would have been hamstrung in his overseas dealings by the existence of the investment currency premium, plus the added aggravation of the 25 per cent 'surrender rule' which was abolished towards the end of 1977.

The investment currency premium is an important concept to understand if you want to engage in direct investment overseas, because the premium is not on the overseas share price but on the investment currency which has to be bought separately and then used to buy your overseas shares.

The rationale for the premium's existence is to be found in the Second World War, when all UK investments overseas were frozen and the British Government took over the power to sell foreign shares itself to finance the enormous cost of the war. Such was the drain of the war that it was found necessary to erect a 'fence' around the UK by safeguarding the country's foreign currency reserves which were needed to purchase all important raw materials and other essential imports during the post-war era. Under the Foreign Exchange Act of 1947 investors were allowed to buy foreign investments outside the sterling area only if there was a matching sale, so that there was no drain on the official currency reserves. The next stage was reached when sales of overseas shares outpaced purchases and brokers were allowed, as a concession, to keep the proceeds of these sales for future re-investment overseas. This was the start of the investment currency 'pool', a new market which depended for its 'price' on the forces of supply and demand. Until 1965 demand was not great and the premium an investor had to pay over and above the market price of his overseas shares never reached more than 6 per cent. Then the Treasury siphoned off some of the pool against the background of the economic crisis of 1965 to inhibit British investment outside the sterling area. The siphoning mechanism was the imposition of the 25 per cent surrender rule. This meant that when an investor eventually sold his overseas investments he was not allowed to convert all the proceeds back at the investment currency rate: 25 per cent of the foreign currency proceeds had to be sold back at the official rate of exchange. This was the rule which Chancellor Healey ended at the latter end of 1977 after a strong inflow into sterling.

The investment currency premium itself has remained, and has reached very high levels both in the traumatic years between 1974 and 1977, when investors sought to diversify their share portfolios away from the crisis-racked UK, and during years when sterling slipped steadily away in value against other, 'hard' trading currencies.

This slipping away has caused some confusion in the minds of many an investor because the investment currency premium is quoted both on a nominal basis and at an effective rate. The 'nominal' investment currency premium is calculated on the basis of £1 = $2.60. It is a simple enough matter to convert the nominal rate into the effective rate, however, by merely looking up the 'conversion factor' which is published daily, under the American Stocks column in the *Financial Times* Share Information Service.

For example if the nominal rate was, say, 55 per cent and the conversion factor was 0.7599 this would give an effective investment currency premium of 55%×0.7599=41.79%.

While the arithmetic is simple enough, judgement is more difficult because the existence of the investment currency premium adds another catch if you want to invest directly in overseas markets. You have to make up your mind about not only the probabilities of a particular share going up, but also (and even if your overseas share does go up in price) the possibility of your losing money on the investment currency premium. For example, after the 25 per cent surrender rule was abolished in mid-December 1977 the effective investment currency premium (or, colloquially, the 'dollar premium') nose-dived from 40 to 30 per cent at the end of the month. This movement was essentially caused by the weakness of the dollar which exacerbated a notoriously volatile dollar premium market. Since the size of the liquid investment currency pool fluctuates between just £50 million and £150 million, UK investors do not have to sell much of their overseas portfolios – estimated at £8.2 billion at the end of 1976 – to have a significant impact on the investment currency premium. The lower the premium falls, the more attractive overseas investment becomes, but this in turn touches off another psychological scare in the market place. As the premium falls, so do the rumours grow in the market place that it will be abolished. In which case, why pay even 25 per cent or 30 per cent over the odds if you aren't going to get it back?

THE MANAGED FUND – THE ROUTE ROUND THE PREMIUM

The private investor has, of course, an alternative to paying the investment currency premium because he or she can buy units in a unit trust which is set up primarily to invest in overseas markets or in an investment trust which is structured to do the same. Not that this is the only reason why such unit trusts and investment trusts are set up, but they can by-pass the premium in the way that a private investor cannot.

Investment trust companies can borrow in foreign currencies to buy overseas shares, thereby avoiding paying the premium, but it is worth pointing out that the investment trust company concerned must maintain a margin equivalent to 15 per cent of the amount borrowed which must be purchased and maintained in premium and loan investment.

Unit trusts can only raise 'reciprocal loans' for overseas investment, and these involve making an equivalent amount of sterling available in the UK to the lender.

Another device which is used by the institutional overseas investor such as an investment trust, a device which is not available to the private UK citizen, is to interpose a holding company in a low-tax haven in order to defer liability to tax on income from overseas investments.

UNIT TRUST PERFORMANCE

As we have already seen in chapter 2, the investor who allots part of his cash to a unit trust whether investing in the UK or overseas, has to suffer an immediate drop in the value of his capital due to front-end loading at the time of purchasing the units. This means that the unit trust performance has to be good enough to make up the initial loss, plus the on-going management fee, and deliver additional capital appreciation on top. How have overseas-oriented unit trusts – of which there are many – actually fared?

The results show that the lesson spelled out earlier – that investment in shares, whether direct or through units, calls for constant switching if the investor is to be successful – remains good. The trouble is, of course, that such switching is difficult in the world of unit trusts because the front-end loading element makes them suitable for the long-term holder who can spread his initial expenses over a period of years. Take 1977, for example, a year in which the UK stock market registered the biggest rise, while the US and the Japanese markets put up a poor performance. As a result M & G Recovery Unit Trust topped the league tables prepared by *Planned Savings.* Of the bottom five performers, three were specialists in North America and were caught out by the fall of Wall Street during 1977, while the other two were invested in the Far East. The top American trust was GT US & General which registered a tiny 2 per cent capital appreciation as against M & G Recovery's 115 per cent rate of growth. Yet Wall Street is the biggest overseas stock market as far as the UK investor is concerned, and there is an embarrassment of choice of unit trusts oriented towards this market as this list of unit trusts investing in North America shows (source: *Unit Trust Year Book 1977*): Piccadilly American Fund; National Westminster Universal; Arbuthnot North America; Bishopsgate International; Britannia North American; GT US & General; Gartmore American; Grantchester; Hambro Securities of America; Henderson North American; Hill Samuel Dollar; Ionian Foreign; Lawson American; M & G American & General; S & P US Growth; Stewart American; Trident American Growth; Unicorn American; Rowan American Fund; Crescent International; S & P Universal Growth (30% USA); S & P Select International (27% USA): National Westminster Growth Investment (up to 34% N. America); Midland Drayton International (36% N. America).

However, a unit trust manager could equally turn round and say that a comparison during a single year is unfair, sustained performance being the criterion which counts. If one evaluates the performance of unit trusts involved in overseas markets from 1971 to 1976, one discovers that, over that six-year period, S & P Japan Growth had shown the highest rate of capital appreciation (+264 per cent), while over a four-year period, 1973–6, Hill Samuel Dollar came second top of the league with an 84 per cent growth rate. Yet over the six-year period during which S & P Japan Growth notched up the highest growth record (according to *Planned Savings*) Lawson American were second bottom of the league, dropping 35 per cent over the period. Had you invested £100 on 1 July 1977 in M & G Far Eastern, your investment would have comfortably increased to £146.70, M & G Far Eastern being the top performing overseas oriented unit trust during the first half of 1978. The lesson to be learned is that if the investor does not wish to deal direct in overseas markets, using his own judgement, it is best for him to select a trust showing sustained performance over a period of years, and not select one trust on the basis of a single year's performance. But there is also considerable opportunity, despite the costs of dealing between unit trusts, for switching between trusts focussing on different economies.

INVESTMENT TRUSTS

The majority of investment trusts invest some of their funds abroad. In recent years a number of investment trust companies have been set up to invest exclusively overseas, but investment abroad is nothing new for the old established companies, which over the years have built up considerable expertise in foreign investment, particularly in the USA. One analysis shows that of total investment trust company assets of about £4,000 million, over one-third is invested in overseas stock markets, mostly in the USA. Here is a list of some of the investment trusts with a significant American link: American Trust; Atlantic Assets Trust; British, American & General Trust; Edinburgh American Assets; First Scottish American Trust; London Atlantic; Montagu Boston; New York & Gartmore; Northern American. And so the list goes on, with other investment trusts specializing in the Japanese or European markets.

As we have already seen in chapter 3, investment trusts generally suffer from the fact that the share price stands at a discount to the net asset value of the trusts' holding of shares because the supply of investment trust shares exceeds demand. The reason for the over-supply is to be found in disenchantment with investment trusts generally, given the greater attractions (and the more heavily marketed) unit trusts. Further, the big institutions no longer use investment trusts as a way to diversify their funds out of the UK. The only stimulus to the market is the possibility of a takeover bid being mounted for a trust by an institutional investor anxious to pick up a large portfolio of shares at less than the price he would have to pay for the same shares in the open market. A sustained upsurge in a particular market – such as that of the US or Japan – would create a welcome opportunity for the investor seeking to diversify his portfolio out of the UK and wishing to buy shares in a professionally managed investment trust.

Chapter 9

Gilt-Edged Investments

The lesson to be learned from the history of investment in gilt-edged stocks is that the long-term holder, who buys for income and then settles back to collect year in year out, loses money. Long-term holders of Government stock who may have bought in the 1940s, 1950s and early 1960s will have seen a substantial proportion of their capital wiped out both in nominal terms – because the price of Government stock has sunk steadily as interest rates have risen – and also in real terms because of inflation. After a period of disillusionment, investors returned to the gilt market in substantial numbers in 1976 and 1977, lured by the attraction of high interest rates.

There is money to be made from gilts, whether you want income, capital gains or a combination of both, but only if you operate a proper gilt-edged investment policy. If you do not like the headaches attendant on carrying out your own gilt investment policy, there are gilt-edged funds which will do the job for you.

BACKGROUND

Gilt-edged stock is issued periodically by the UK Government when it needs funds. Stock is issued with a fixed or floating coupon or rate of interest, and the par value of the stocks is paid at redemption (ie. you collect £100 for every £100 nominal).

Until the mid-fifties, Government stock was the bulwark of the investment market. Respectable investors, whether private or corporate, relied mainly on gilts as the major investment sector open to them. Ordinary shares, even in a publicly quoted company, were for the speculative investor. Consequently, companies had to pay a much higher rate of dividend than was provided by gilts because the latter could offer the investor complete security. Today the position is reversed, and yields on gilts can offer double the yield provided by ordinary shares. The other factor to remember is that for twenty years after the last war, the 'natural' rate of interest was thought of as 2½ per cent. When interest rates started creeping up to the 6 and 7 per cent mark there were howls of anguish, which may seem ludicrous to us now, with Minimum Lending Rate having touched 15 per cent in the autumn of 1976. The 1960s and (particularly) the 1970s witnessed gilt yields being forced higher and higher (and prices dropping lower and lower) due to the twin stimuli of ever-increasing interest rates – allied to the Government need to raise money with which to finance public sector expenditure – and ever-increasing rates of inflation.

WHY DO INVESTORS BUY GILTS?

First, there is the sweetener that if you hold gilts longer than a year, there is no liability to capital gains tax, unlike equities. If you buy gilts which are on the National Savings Register (forms for this are available at Post Offices) income is paid gross before tax, but you can only buy £5,000 nominal of any one stock at any one time.

Second, interest rates can move down as well as up. So individuals and institutions, particularly insurance companies, need the essential factor of certainty for their calculations. By buying gilts giving a guaranteed yield of, say 11 per cent over a seven-year period it is possible to match the maturity date with some other aspect of investment (perhaps the provision of an annuity) with complete certainty. Equally, an individual requiring the assurance of a guaranteed income for the rest of his life of, say, 14 per cent, could buy undated Government stock. Both the insurance company and the individual are protected against any further interest rate changes. If the interest rate structure moves down, then they still get their 11 per cent and 14 per cent respectively. If the interest rates move further up then they still have the same certainty, except that they have lost the opportunity of achieving an even higher yield. You cannot get this certainty from the volatile, short-term money markets.

The other reason for buying gilts is capital gain. If interest rates move down, the investor can sell his gilts for a capital gain (alternatively, if interest rates move further up then a capital loss is accrued). Both capital gains and capital losses are chargeable, and offsettable, against capital gains tax if gilts are bought and sold within a year.

A WORKED EXAMPLE

Let us work through a potential optimised profit, selecting for our purposes Treasury 11½% 1981 and let us assume we hold the stock for over twelve months (thus avoiding capital gains tax liability) and receive two coupons.

Buying price	89⅝ cum dividend
Selling price	103¾₁₆ ex dividend
Capital profit	13.94 points
Equivalent gross (assuming standard rate of tax of 33%)	13.94×100/67=20.81 points
Income (less standard rate of tax)	12.83*×67/100=8.60 points
Total return (20.81+8.60)	=29.41 points (+33%)

*100−11½/89⅝=12.83

The astute reader will have noticed from the example above that most of the yield comes from capital gain. As one goes up the tax scale, so does the income element from gilts drop and the capital gains attractions – when grossed up to allow for the fact that the capital profit is tax-free – increase.

The rewards of operating a shrewd gilt-edged switching policy can be very great if the investor gets his buying and selling decisions right. Bear in mind that the longer the date of the gilt-edged stock and the lower the coupon, the greater is the price movement in response to a change in the yield structure. Another change which took place in the structure of the gilt market at the beginning of the 1970s was a realisation of the importance of equivalent gross yields. Prices of low-coupon stocks (where the capital profit component of the yield was greater) rose faster than the high-coupon stocks. This was especially marked in the low-coupon, medium-dated gilt-edged stock sector. A specialised market in low-coupon stocks emerged with one very important factor in its favour. 'Tap' stock issues carried increasingly higher coupons. The low-coupon stocks still in issue today are a hangover from low-interest rate eras, and the amount in issue is steadily being reduced by redemptions. Excluding undated stocks the nominal amount in issue of low-coupon stocks (below 5 per cent) in 1971 was £5,104 million. By 1976 this had dropped to £3,362 million and by 1981 the total will be down to £1,750 million. This represents a sector of the gilt-edged market where supply does not increase, but is steadily going down, while demand from taxpayers can – when the prospects look bright and interest rates look like moving down – be high. Low-coupon gilts are particularly attractive to investors in high tax brackets for the very good reason that all gilts are free of capital gains tax if held for over one year.

LONGER-TERM GILTS

In the case of longer-term gilt-edged stocks, the situation is rather different because stocks in this category are bought for their tax advantages and are affected by investors' expectations as to the future rate of inflation. Demand for the high-coupon stocks is maintained to a substantial extent by the cash flow of the pension funds and insurance companies which are always potential buyers of these investments. While shorter-dated stocks cannot free themselves from the countervailing influences of money market rates, longer-dated gilts are influenced to a much greater extent by the expectations of the institutional investment managers who are prepared to look beyond short-run circumstances. In this sector the investor may be prepared to accept the risk of a long-dated security, despite the fact that the improvement in circumstances which has led him to buy may be several months away.

For those prepared to take the risk that interest rates will fall, the rewards are very high. At present 'real' interest rates at the undated end of the gilt market are about negative if we allow for inflation and tax. But if long-term interest rates fell by 30 per cent over the next three years – from, say, 16 per cent to 11 per cent – gilt prices would rise by 45 per cent. If this very agreeable scenario took place, the investor would find himself still in receipt of a 14 per cent income plus the added bonus that the value of his capital would have risen by half as much again.

POLITICAL CONSIDERATIONS

Perhaps this is the point at which also to sound a word of political warning. The cost of funding the national debt by means of gilt issues is now astronomically high compared with the 7 per cent average the Government paid only a few years ago. The Government has to fund its debt regardless of cost, otherwise the country itself would go bankrupt. The money just has to be found to pay out social security benefits, the salaries of those working in the public sector, the Government's investment programme etc. If the money was not there then the Government's position would be exactly the same as that of a bank which has run out of money and has to close its doors. So the Government must turn to a supranational bank for credit (the IMF) and also pay the institutional investment managers the rates of interest (15 per cent or more in the autumn of 1976) required if those managers are to continue to lend to HMG. The introduction of a floating-rate Government stock has been one way of lowering the cost of financing Government debt but floating-rate stocks are unattractive to pension funds and insurance companies (the biggest gilt buyers) because they like to work on the basis of fixed rates in order to get their future sums right.

Remember that if you buy your gilts – through the Post Office, your bank manager, accountant or solicitor – via the National Savings Register route then you collect your interest gross before tax. This appeals not only to the non-taxpayer but also the taxpayer who can put the interest to work until he has to pay his tax bill; it is known as the 'interest on interest' factor.

GILT-EDGED FUNDS

If you want to avoid all the hassle of continually buying and selling in the gilt-edged market, there are investment vehicles known as gilt-edged funds which take the hassle from your shoulders in return for a management fee. Actually, to call them funds is something of a misnomer: they are, in effect, gilt-edged portfolio management services which give private individuals a chance to achieve the same results on the gilt markets as do the big investment institutions. The service involves pooling a large number of relatively small amounts of cash available for gilt-edged investment and treating them as one large fund. The advantages of this pooling arrangement are that the clients get access to investment management which is normally only available to the big institutional funds, and that the economies of scale – in terms of commissions paid and administration costs – can be passed on. The charges to gain access to this gilt-edged management service are 1¼ per cent at the outset and then ½ per cent per annum, with a minimum annual fee of £40–£50. The size of the management fee means that you really need to have at least £5,000 to invest in the fund to make the operation worthwhile.

Every investor who joins the service retains a 'beneficial interest' in his investment and is in much the same position as if he had entrusted his gilt-edged investment portfolio to the fund as a private client. But the fund has full discretion in investment policy on the gilt market and each individual's portfolio is tailored to ensure that a uniform policy is pursued.

In order to provide an 'index of value' the overall gilt-edged portfolio (the master fund) is valued and divided to show the value on a scale based on £100 invested in the master fund (with a £100 invested at the first valuation = 100). The index is then published fortnightly in the *Financial Times* so that each investor can easily establish the approximate value of his portfolio and how well his fund managers are performing on the gilt market.

There is an 'income portfolio' for the standard-rate taxpayer, and a 'capital portfolio' for the higher-rate taxpayer who seeks capital gains rather than income for the obvious tax advantages. There is no minimum amount of money which can be

69

invested in the funds, although the annual minimum manage-ment charge rules out the very small investor. A bank is the custodian of the funds, and income distributions are made twice a year. By the way, a tip worth remembering is that a commission of half the initial charge (less expenses) is usually paid to introductory agents, so it is worth your while to feed your cash through to a gilt-edged fund via your accountants in return for the quid pro quo of reduced accountancy fees to yourself.

Chapter 10

Local Authority Investments

Local authorities are frequently being castigated as the pro-
fligate villains of the national, public-sector, squandering scene.
Even if this is not the place to review the rights and wrongs
of local authority expenditure, very much to the point is where
do local authorities get their money to spend – apart from
your yearly, half-yearly or monthly rates cheque, that is? One
source of their funds is by borrowing from the public: you will
probably have noticed one manifestation of this in the myriad
little box advertisements in the financial sections of the newspapers which read 'City of Birmingham Trustee Bonds, 12%
5 or 6 years, Min. £1,000, Explanatory Leaflet, City Treasurer', or 'Invest in Liverpool, Minimum £500, Interest paid
half yearly, 11½% 2, 3 and 4 years, 12% 5, 6 and 7 years,
Write to the City Treasurer'.

LOCAL AUTHORITIES VERSUS OTHERS

It is worth leaving some money with your bank – in current
account, that is – for the very good reason that if you do not
leave a minimum balance there then you will get stuck for
bank charges: all the banks, with the exception of the Cooperative Bank, make charges if your minimum (or yearly
average) balance falls below a certain figure. Over and above
that minimum balance a good number of people are content
to leave their money on an ordinary deposit account with their
bank. Building societies generally offer higher yields than do
bank deposit accounts – but tax at the standard rate is deducted
at source from building society interest payments. This enables

71

the building societies to put in their advertising that a depositor or investor is earning a much higher yield on a grossed up basis. However, you should bear in mind that no machinery exists for clawing back this tax from the maw of the Inland Revenue if you happen to be a less than standard rate taxpayer.

Local authority bonds are an alternative, high-yielding home for surplus cash. While tax at the standard rate is deducted at source, non-taxpayers and taxpayers under the standard rate can reclaim this tax back from the Inland Revenue. Local authority temporary deposits (up to one year) pay you gross before tax, leaving you to settle your own affairs with the taxman.

LOCAL AUTHORITIES – SECURITY

Before going on to explain the ins and outs of local authority bonds – the types and advantages, the pitfalls and how you go about buying them – and of temporary deposits, let us look into the question of security. After the financial traumas of 1973 and 1974 people are naturally cautious as to where they put their money. 'Will it be safe?' they wonder. Since the recent re-organisation of local authorities their number has been reduced from 1,700 to about 500. No local authority has ever defaulted on its debt and it is inconceivable – although no formal guarantee exists – that Whitehall would allow such a catastrophe to happen. The central government would stand behind any local authority in trouble, while local authorities also have access to the Government-backed Public Works Loan Board. While each local authority is expected to make 'all reasonable efforts' to obtain a pre-determined slice of its financial needs from open market borrowing, if it needs the money and can offer proof that the cash cannot be raised from other sources, the Public Works Loan Board will act as lender of last resort. This is a similar situation to that of the Bank of England which acts as a lender of last resort to the discount houses.

'TOWN HALL' BONDS

There are two types of local authority bonds. First, there are

72

the 'Town Hall', or 'advertised', or 'over the counter' bonds, which are all euphemisms in the trade to describe the bonds you see advertised in your daily newspaper. Tip number one is, if you look at the local authority bonds table offered in a daily newspaper, do not think you are comparing like with like when it comes to interest rates, or that the highest rate of interest necessarily offers you the best deal. Differences in interest rates are accounted for by the different elements in the package the local authority is offering. Thus the bonds may be offered for different lengths of time – for example a bond where you are contractually locking up your money for a minimum of five years obviously offers a higher rate of interest than a bond with a one-year life. And, if you do lock your money up for five years, you could be looking pretty sick if interest rates go through the roof and you are left sitting on a low-yielding investment. Local authorities will on occasion release you from your contractual obligations in the event of premature death or hardship, but they are not keen to do so. Then again, the rate of interest offered could be affected by the size of the minimum sum which the local authority is prepared to take – some take in as little as £200 (and lower the offered rate for these small amounts accordingly) while others only take a minimum of £5,000.

Tip number two is to read the small print. Some local authorities offer to pay interest half-yearly, others only on the maturity of the bond. As the interest paid in the latter case is simple as opposed to compound, then you are losing the 'interest on interest' benefit, although the rate offered should reflect this loss. The rate of interest is fixed for the term of the bond, so you know from the outset just where you are and what income you will certainly receive – unlike the rates offered by building societies or on bank deposits which can be changed as the interest rate structure changes. If rates move down, then you benefit from this certainty. If rates move up then you are left with the knowledge that your capital could be earning more elsewhere.

There are no costs involved in buying a local authority bond of this type. All you have to do is to apply for an application form to the local authority of your choice and, assuming that it is still accepting money on the terms stated in its advertisement, return the form completed together with a cheque. But bear in mind that you should select the bond which is right for your purposes: if you think you will need the money back after a year is up, then go for a one-year bond. If you want peace of mind and the highest obtainable income over a five-year period, then go for a five-year bond – and do not look at the alternative rates obtainable for the next five years just in case interest rates have gone up to such an extent that you fret yourself into an early grave.

NEGOTIABLE BONDS

Negotiable bonds are a different species. These bonds, some-times called 'yearling' bonds because they are normally mature in a year (but can be for longer periods), are issued through and quoted on the Stock Exchange. You can buy them from your bank, through a stockbroker, or through an accountant. Unlike 'advertised' bonds, negotiable bonds incur costs of roughly £5 commission on every £1,000 worth of bonds bought, but this commission reduces the larger the amount of money involved. The point of interest about negotiable bonds is that, unlike the advertised variety, you can sell (and buy) the bonds before maturity as an active 'secondary' market in the bonds is maintained by the discount houses and other financial institutions. The rate of interest on the bonds moves in line with general money market rates. Tip number three therefore is a tax tip. If you are a higher rate taxpayer, then it is worth thinking about negotiable bonds because they do offer the opportunity of making a capital gain and capital gains tax is a good deal less than income tax. You can sell the bonds 'full of interest' before interest becomes due and thus convert income into capital gain. But be warned. If the Inland Revenue feel you are carrying out this practice over-frequently they can treat your capital gain as income from trading and tax it accordingly. Negotiable bonds are dealt in from a minimum amount of £1,000 and upwards, and they are issued for periods of one to five years. Interest, which is normally paid half-yearly, is payable net after standard rate of tax, which if you are a less than standard rate taxpayer can be reclaimed.

TEMPORARY DEPOSITS

Normally local authorities will take only sums of £20,000 plus on temporary deposit and you will earn slightly more than from a special deposit with your bank (special deposits are taken if the sum involved is over £10,000). Interest is payable gross. A small number of local authorities are prepared to accept loans for from 7 days to 364 days in relatively small sums.

If you want to obtain a full list of local authority bonds – free – this can be obtained from the Loans Bureau of the Chartered Institute of Public Finance and Accountancy, 238 Vauxhall Bridge Road, London SW1V 1AN (please send s.a.e.), who will also deal with telephone enquiries on 01-828 7855 after 3.30 p.m.

LOCAL AUTHORITY 'FLOATERS'

The summer of 1977 witnessed the development of new instruments on the local authority investment scene: the local authority floating-rate stock and the local authority floating-rate negotiable bond. Taking a lead from the UK Government, the local authorities launched stock issues with the interest rate offered to investors so structured that it floated up or down with prevailing money market rates. The Government floating-rate gilt-edged stock had been launched earlier with a rate of interest pegged to the Treasury Bill Rate. The first local authority stock issue – for Bristol – emulated this example by linking the coupon on this £10 million stock issue, maturing in 1982, to the Treasury Bill Rate. The margin over the Treasury Bill Rate was 1½ per cent, which contrasts with the first floating-rate gilt-edged stock which had a margin of a mere ½ per cent. This formula was quickly abandoned in favour of linking the stock issues to the six-months London Interbank Offered Rate. Initially – for the Dudley and Oldham stock issues of £10 million apiece – the 'spread' over the six-months LIBOR was 1 per cent. Pressure of demand (both the Dudley and Oldham stock issues were heavily oversubscribed) led to the spread being cut to ¾ per cent for succeeding issues.

The stock issues were primarily designed for institutional

deposit takers like banks and building societies, although the latter had to wait for the Treasury to amend the regulations in order to enable them to buy the new floating-rate local authority stock issues.

However, the increasing flow of issues has resulted in a large new market developing in this medium-maturity local authority investment which can be bought and sold on the secondary market in the City of London. Pember & Boyle, the stock-brokers, and Morgan Grenfell, the merchant bank, played leading roles in introducing and developing the market.

The local authorities' floating-rate negotiable bonds, which were launched in the autumn of 1977, proved to be rather a different kettle of fish. While designed primarily for the banking community they can also be of interest to private investors seeking the protection of a floating rate at a time when the investor believes that the UK interest rate structure will move up in a sustained way. For years the local authorities had been trying to get the Bank of England to allow them to issue local authority certificates of deposit to enable local authorities to tap new sources of short-term, comparatively low-cost cash. The Bank of England had always fought shy – given its rather traumatic experiences with the sterling certificate of deposit market in 1972 and 1973 – of adding a new, possibly unstable and inflationary instrument to the money market scene. And it must be remembered that local authorities have no power to issue bearer documents, which a certificate of deposit would have been, nor can local authorities pay interest gross to non-banking lenders unless they are granted exemption.

By way of compromise, the Bank allowed the local authorities to issue floating-rate negotiable bonds (bonds, by the way, are issued for periods of five years or less, while stocks are issued for periods of more than five years). After permission was given there was a spate of five-year negotiable bonds issued with an interest rate spread of ¾ per cent over the six-months London Interbank Offered Rate. The first three-year floating-rate bond, which had a spread of ⅝ per cent over the six-months LIBOR did not go down too well in the market.

The drawback to the floating-rate bond is that interest is paid net after standard rate income tax, so the investor loses the 'interest on interest' benefit he or she gets when interest is paid gross as it is with bank deposits or with local authority temporary deposits. The advantage of the bonds is that they do provide the investor with protection against an upward movement in interest rates because his income will rise in parallel. In addition the bonds are highly liquid – they can be bought and sold in the 'secondary' market at any time. This gives them a marked advantage over the local authority fixed-rate, advertised bonds which lock up the investor's cash for periods of one to five years.

Chapter 11

Successful Investment with Britain's Building Societies

Curiously enough, given the simple nature of the building society concept, investment with Britain's building societies is one of the least understood of the investment sectors. Even sophisticated investors, who have mastered the intricacies of, say, the options market, can be baffled when it comes to threading their way through the maze of different investment packages offered by Britain's 250 plus building societies. 'Ordinary' shares, 'subscription' shares, 'term' shares, 'preference' shares, 'contract' shares, 'bonus' shares can be baffling enough to the man in the street, but on top of this plethora of names is piled all the differences between the individual building societies themselves in terms of the minimum amounts of money which particular building societies will accept, and of the differing lengths of time for which the investor's cash is locked up in particular types of investment schemes.

On the whole, the system appears to work well enough despite its intricacy. This is really due to the fact that the building societies see their investors as dividing into two sectors.

A HOME FOR SURPLUS CASH

The first sector tends to be made up of those members of the general public who use building societies as homes for surplus cash building up a reserve cushion to be drawn upon when needed. This sector itself splits into two parts. The first part would comprise what used to be called 'blue-collar workers' who may not have a clearing bank account. In fact, only 40 per cent of the working population does have a clearing bank account, so this leaves a very substantial number of income earners who need to find homes for their surplus cash. A few years ago, blue-collar workers would have been referred to by statisticians as the C and D income groups, differentiating them from the A and B income groups which comprised the higher-income middle and upper middle classes. However, inflation, wage and salary restraints and the incidence of taxation have put paid to such neat dividing lines. In many cases, the beleaguered middle managers with, say, B classification life-styles have been overtaken in income terms by the higher paid blue-collar workers. The latter tend to have two advantages over the lower paid middle manager. One is that if overtime is worked, it is paid for, whereas if a middle manager works overtime it tends to be on an unpaid basis. In fact, a recent survey estimated that Britain's middle managers worked overtime to the tune of £3,000 a year each but without, of course, reaping the material reward for their collective zeal. The other advantage is that the middle manager's life-style (and, indeed the life style of the A and B income groups) tends to demand an ownership of a house with the concomitant requirement for a mortgage, which needs servicing from current income for so long as the mortgage period lasts. Even after tax allowances for mortgage interest repayments, the borrower still has a monthly burden – sometimes a very substantial burden at that – on his shoulders. Historically, the blue-collar worker, whether from inertia, belief or inherited habit, has preferred rented accommodation. In that the private landlords' sector of rented accommodation has enormously reduced in size, this usually means that the blue-collar worker will be paying a council-controlled rent which will encompass a fairly substantial subsidy. Some idea of the enormous change which has taken place in the housing market since 1951 is shown in Table 6.

Table 6. *Housing Ownership 1951–76*

	1951	1976
Stock of dwellings	14.3 million	20.6
Owner occupied	29%	53%
Rented from local authorities	18%	32%

This means that many a blue-collar worker has higher 'discretionary' income (ie. income left to spend after meeting any standard, month by month commitments such as mortgage) than many a middle manager with, ostensibly, higher income. This trend is particularly marked in Scotland in which home ownership financed by mortgage is less than that of the rest of the country.

This surplus cash of the blue-collar worker, who lacks a clearing bank account, will tend to find its way into the local High Street branch of the Trustee Savings Banks – which have cheque-cashing facilities and pay deposit interest rates – or into the local building society. On the whole, savers in this category are more interested in convenience of location and ease of withdrawal than with the different interest rates offered by one building society as against another.

A RESERVE CUSHION

The second part of the first group comprises those members of the A and B income groups who have clearing bank accounts but also have surplus cash which they may want to use as a reserve cushion against payment of tax (if they have unearned income), or against payment of tax and VAT (if they are self-employed), or just because they want to keep a reserve cushion of funds available against contingencies. Although no statistical material is available for this hypothesis it is probable that these depositors are more 'interest rate sensitive' than the blue-collar worker. For example, they may well keep a reserve cushion of cash in a bank deposit as well as in a building society. If the rate of interest on their bank deposit drops to an uncompetitively low rate as against a building society deposit rate (which happened in 1977 when the banks were offering 4 per cent gross before tax while the building societies were offering 7 per cent *net* after the standard rate of tax, which grossed up to 12 per cent (more of this grossing up later) then the depositors of this type will be encouraged to switch from bank deposits to building societies. Likewise, the reverse movement can take place, and depositors will switch from building societies into bank deposits, which happened in the autumn of 1977. However, the differential between the rates offered by building societies and by banks seems to have to be reasonably large in order to encourage large-scale switching. On the whole, it may not be worth the effort for the odd half per cent.

THE WHOLESALE MARKET

The other section with which the building societies concern themselves makes up what can only be termed the 'wholesale market'. The funds of this section are controlled by solicitors, accountants and stockbrokers, and include also the surplus cash held by wealthy private investors, which are sensitive to differentials in interest rates between different money market sectors, and between one building society and the next. In the case of the professional advisers, there is a definite incentive to pass funds held in their care temporarily (for example house mortgage funds pending completion, or funds being accumulated before the final disposition of a will) because the building societies pay introductory commission for these wholesale, temporary funds. The commission ranges from ¾ per cent to 1 per cent, so on a deposit of, say, £16,000 a firm of solicitors could expect to receive £160. In the case of the wealthy individual who has, say, over £10,000 to invest in the way of surplus cash, the wholesale inter-bank market is open to him if he wishes to make a 'special deposit'. And special deposits of £10,000 plus always earn much higher rates than ordinary seven-day deposits; usually the gap is 4 per cent or more. In the autumn of 1976, the banks were paying well over 14 per cent for special deposits of this type, so there was an obvious differential over the building society rate at the time (7½ per cent net after tax, or 11.54 per cent gross before tax). Added to this was the fact that the banks do not deduct tax at source, leaving the recipient to earn 'interest on interest' until his tax bill becomes due. As has been seen, the reverse situation happened in 1977, when the special deposit rate fell to 4 per cent gross, while the building societies were still offering 7 per cent net after tax. Such a spread between rates cannot be ignored, and massive switching by the wholesale market took place from bank deposits to building societies.

THE BUILDING SOCIETIES AS LENDERS

The building society movement started off back in the last century as working men's cooperative housing movements. Essentially, this is still their role today except that the tax advantage of a mortgage arrangement, added to the Englishman's desire to own his own particular house and plot of land, has converted the lending aspect of the building society activities largely into a middle-class preserve. However, the societies still have most of their 18 million investors among the working and lower middle classes. So far as the lending aspect is concerned, building society mortgages are remarkably cheap. Britain's best blue-chip companies, such as ICI or Marks and Spencer, could not borrow twenty- and twenty-five-year money at the rate of interest charged to the private individual for a house mortgage over the same term, but when building society mortgage rates go up by say, 1 per cent (and each time the building societies make a rate change it costs them some £15 million in administration) there are usually howls of execration, and political pressure is brought to bear in advance of any such momentous decision. Yet the rational argument would be that a building society mortgage rate of say 11 per cent, after allowing for tax relief and after allowing for inflation, is a negative rate of interest. The money is being invested in a house whose price, given the housing market's experience over the last twenty years or so, will outdistance the rate of inflation, and the increase in the value of the owner's equity in the house is all his – the building society takes no part in it. It is a curious quirk of the English that, while they can pay credit card borrowing rates and hire purchase rates of well over 20 per cent with complete equanimity, they regard a building society interest rate of 10–12 per cent as a thorn in the flesh. Building societies do not see their main rationale in life as making a profit. If they did, they would not be lending twenty-five-year money to private individuals at far cheaper rates than to (ostensibly) much more creditworthy large companies. The main weakness of the building society movement appears to be a pre-occupation with the assets on their balance sheets, and the proliferation of their branch networks. One is tempted to wonder whether this pre-occupation with size corresponds to the very human failing that their Chief General Managers and Boards of Directors want to move higher in the pecking order of the building society league table. The only area in which building societies can exercise their profit-making abilities is with the up to 20 per cent of their assets which they must hold as liquid reserves. With this 20 per cent they can play the money markets and buy short-dated gilt-edged stock to their heart's content. And, of course, they can make much more money from this money manipulation than they do from house mortgages.

The other important fact about the building societies, so far as the public is concerned, is that they look to be as secure as the Bank of England. The Building Societies Association, which was established in 1869, has a membership of 252 building societies throughout the UK. The combined assets of these societies (£21,500 million) represent over 99 per cent of the total funds of all building societies. To be a member of the Association, a building society has to comply to strict financial standards, and even after admission to the Association the annual accounts of every member society are periodically examined to ensure that the Association's regulations are complied with and that the members are conducting their financial affairs with 'a high degree of prudence'. When there is a whiff of mistrust about, the building societies rush to help each other as demonstrated by the case of the Grays Building Society in the early Spring of 1978. This was also amply demonstrated when Rolls Royce was allowed to go bust and there was a run on the company's local building society wherein many of the workers kept their savings. Pledges of support for the beleaguered building society came from other building societies within hours, and the run was checked in its tracks.

'GROSSING UP'

Building societies are taxed on the interest they receive from investments under a special arrangement with the Inland Revenue. Investors receive their interest from building societies with income tax (at the basic tax rate) having been deducted at source. It is important to realise that no machinery exists to enable the investor to recover this tax deducted at source

83

if the investor is not liable for basic rate tax. Tax deducted at source from interest payable on local authority bonds or gilts or from dividends on shares can be reclaimed from the Revenue.

This leaves the building societies with the problem of having to market their wares on a 'grossed up' (ie. after adding back basic rate tax) basis. For example, a rate of interest of 7.8 per cent would be advertised as a 'grossed up' rate of 11.64 per cent. The figure can be worked out easily enough by dividing the net rate of interest offered by the building society by 0.67 (since the current basic rate of tax is 33 per cent).

Investors who are liable to tax at a higher rate need to be aware of the grossed up figure because, unlike those investors paying tax at the basic rate, they have to pay extra tax on their building society interest, based on the grossed up figure. Table 7 shows the effect of taxation on different investment sectors.

Table 7. *How Your Tax Rate Affects Yields*

The table shows what two investment sectors give you by way of return *after tax*, depending on your marginal rate of tax.

Tax rate	National Savings Certificates (14th issue)	Building Societies (Ordinary Deposit Account)
Nil	7.59%	6.7%
33% (standard rate)	7.59%	6.7%
45%	7.59%	5.5%
55%	7.59%	4.5%
65%	7.59%	3.5%
75%	7.59%	2.5%
83%	7.59%	1.7%

The moral: net returns from various investment sectors vary very substantially when you take tax into account.

TYPES OF BUILDING SOCIETY INVESTMENT

The list of names used by building societies to attract investment funds illustrates in itself the main reason why so many savers get bewildered. There are 'shares', 'preference shares', 'contract shares', 'bonus shares', 'term shares', 'monthly income bonds', 'monthly income shares', 'quarterly income shares', 'deposits', 'special deposits', 'advance interest deposits' – and there are also other names invented by particular building societies with which to encourage the saver.

However, for the purposes of investment, building society opportunities can be classified into three broad sectors. First, there are deposit accounts which are the basic foundations of building society investment. They offer the saver freedom to make deposits into his or her account and to withdraw them at any time. Some astute investors have not been slow to cotton on to the fact that this freedom of deposit and withdrawal, plus the fact that a rate of interest is always paid, make the building societies a much more attractive home for salaries and wages than is provided by the clearing banks. The clearing banks offer no rate of interest for funds held on current accounts, and impose charges if balances fall below a pre-determined level.

Next, for the regular saver the building societies offer 'share accounts', such as 'subscription shares' which are monthly savings schemes. The building societies like the guarantee of a regular flow of funds into their coffers and are prepared to pay a higher interest rate to the regular saver. However, the regulations governing subscription shares – as to the amount which can be saved every month – vary from society to society. For example, the saver might be restricted to investing only £8 per month, and once he has accumulated £100 the cash would then have to be transferred to an 'ordinary' share account.

'Term shares' are lump sum investments, under which savers must deposit their money with the building society of their choice for a set, contractual period. As a rule, the longer the term the higher the rate of interest offered. The interest paid can vary ('variable term shares') when there is a change in the Building Societies Association recommended rate during the period when your funds are locked up. As with subscription shares, different building societies have different regulations as to the minimum sum of money accepted (from £100 to £1,000 and more), and as to the varying lengths of time required under the contractual arrangement. A word of caution on term share investment: make sure that you will not need the money you are locking up until maturity. Building societies will only release funds earlier in exceptional circumstances.

By the way, the ceiling for investment in any one building society is £15,000 (or £30,000 for joint accounts), and you can of course have a number of different building society accounts.

Chapter 12

National Savings – Worth Looking Into

There are only two current opportunities open to the UK investor which will guarantee him or her against the ravages of inflation. Every other savings sector, whether it be gilt-edged stock, bank deposits, local authority bonds or any of the other savings opportunities designed to appeal to those seeking income, including the building societies, offers the saver a negative return as long as inflation outpaces the rate of interest offered. Work it out for yourself. If inflation is running at 12 per cent and your gilt-edged stock yields a gross of tax income of 11 per cent then you are losing money even before tax is taken into account.

Unless you can make substantial capital gains, which always involves taking a measure of risk, the real value of your capital must inevitably go down in an age of inflation. There are only two, small, public sector investment opportunities which offer the investor the chance to keep his capital at the same level (but without providing a real rate of return over and above this level). These are the inflation-proofed Retirement Certificates which allow a holding of £700 but are only available to pensioners. The other is the Save-As-You-Earn, index-linked, National Savings scheme, where the maximum monthly contribution is £20. The British Government was reluctantly forced into offering these index-linked schemes because granting protection to the few weakens demands for protection to the many. After all, if the British Government accepted the principle of equity during an age of rip-roaring inflation, it would have to concede the case for indexing tax, wages, salaries, mortgages. If inflation is running at well into double figures, as was the case in 1975-7, the monetary consequences for the Treasury would be cataclysmic if indexation were applied to all monetary transactions. When inflation is reduced to manageable proportions, producing a climate under which such an indexation scheme could be implemented, then the Government could always argue that the need for such indexation had disappeared along with the inflationary climate.

THE NATIONAL SAVINGS MOVEMENT

The National Savings Bank was first established back in the 1880s and it still, today, sticks to the principles upon which it was first founded, to cater for the needs of the working man who wished to put away present income for future use. And with a substantial proportion of the working population today not having the benefits of clearing bank accounts, together with the money transmission facility of the cheque book, the National Savings Bank and the Trustee Savings Banks still look after the needs of the great mass of the saving population, including schoolchildren. It is worth making a brief aside here to point out that the Trustee Savings Banks, which are area banks run on federal lines, are trying to become to all intents and purposes clearing banks akin to Barclays or the National Westminster. The Trustee Savings Banks are offering their customers cheque book facilities, and there are also unit trust and insurance schemes on offer through the TSB Trust Company. The National Savings movements in Britain is run by the Department of National Savings in liaison with the Treasury, and it is worth remembering that National Savings constitute a cheap money inflow to the Treasury's coffers so the Treasury takes a leading role in establishing the terms to be offered to savers.

From approaching an inflow of £1 billion in 1972–3, National Savings slumped away to an inflow of some £200 million in the financially traumatic year of 1973–4. It has since climbed steadily from approaching £500 million in 1974–5 to over £750 million in 1975–6, followed by a massive leap to nearly £1½ billion in 1976–7 and another increase to

£1.9 million in 1977–8. This compares with a net receipt figure for the building society movement of approaching £2½ billion in the same year.

The reason why there was such a big inflow into National Savings during 1976–7 was not because the savers for whom the National Savings movement was designed had been saving more; on the contrary, the proportion of saving to income steadily slipped away in 1976–7 as workers, managers and the retired dipped into their savings in order to maintain their standard of living against the harsh background of high inflation and wages and dividends curbs. The real reason for the boom in National Savings was that the wily institutional investors – building societies, or charities for example – and the more astute private investors who nipped into National Savings Certificates in the spring of 1977 when interest rates started dropping like a stone, recognised their chance to get a high rate of interest while the going was good and took it. Those who bought the 16th issue of National Savings Certificates, when they were on issue from mid-December 1976 to the end of March 1977, were left sitting comfortably on a net income of almost 8.8 per cent over four years.

By jumping ahead to the 16th issue of National Savings Certificates we are in danger of starting at the tail end of this chapter instead of at the beginning. So let's hark back to the bedrock of the movement – the National Savings Bank. Together, the Trustee Savings Banks and the schemes administered by the Department for National Savings account for £15.7 billion in savings and deposits. Excluding the Trustee Savings Banks' figures, National Savings totalled £10.3 billion at the end of May 1978 – a figure which compares with £6.3 billion at the end of March 1972. The National Savings Bank itself accounts for £3.3 billion of the total in the form of deposits left on ordinary account and in the longer term investment account. The entry point to the National Savings Bank is through the Post Office; in fact the voluntary National Savings groups now only provide under 6½ per cent of gross National Savings inflows, the balance coming through the entry points of the Post Office, the Trustee Savings Bank and the clearing banks.

THE ORDINARY ACCOUNT

The National Savings Bank ordinary account can offer the investor an attractive alternative to leaving his or her surplus cash within the clearing bank deposit accounts because it can offer a higher rate of interest. For example, in the autumn of 1977, when clearing banks offered a minuscule 3 per cent for deposit funds, the National Savings Bank ordinary account offered 5 per cent. There are important tax sweeteners to the National Savings ordinary account which can render them attractive. There is a tax exemption of £70 which applies equally across all rates of tax. What this tax exemption boils down to in practice is that a depositor can leave £1,400 on deposit with the National Savings Bank and pay no tax on the interest (£70 being 5 per cent of £1,400). The National Savings ordinary account is the first introduction which schoolchildren have to saving: you can open an account if you are over seven. And you can deposit sums of 25p, up to a maximum total of £10,000, but societies (such as building societies) and other organisations which handle large funds can apply to exceed the limit of £10,000.

INVESTMENT ACCOUNTS

National Savings investment accounts are designed for the longer-term holder because you have to give one calendar month's notice of withdrawal. While the interest paid on investment accounts was reduced by 1 per cent on 1 October 1977 from 10 per cent to 9 per cent (and subsequently to 8½ per cent), the rate still offered a hefty premium above the deposit rate offered by the banking system at that time and compared quite well against the rate offered on ordinary accounts by building societies; the Building Societies Association recommended net rate of interest was 6 per cent in the autumn of 1977 which grossed up to 9.09 per cent giving those building societies offering the recommended rate a tiny .09 per cent edge. Normally, the National Savings interest rate structure is slow to move up when interest rates are rising nationally, and equally slow to come down when interest rates are dropping. You can open a National Savings investment account with only £1 but you can hold a maximum of £50,000. This maximum limit was imposed in July 1977, but you can maintain deposits of over £50,000 provided that the deposits were build up before the ceiling was imposed.

While up to £30 can be withdrawn on demand at a Savings Bank Post Office from a National Savings ordinary account, one month's notice of withdrawal is required on investment accounts. Interest on the latter, by the way, is paid gross before tax, so an investment account is obviously superior to a building society account for the non-standard-rate taxpayer or for those who prefer to settle their own affairs with HM Inspector of Taxes. Building societies deduct tax from interest payments at the standard rate at source, and no machinery exists for reclaiming this tax from the Revenue if you have no standard-rate tax liability.

NATIONAL SAVINGS CERTIFICATES

Apart from the straightforward National Savings ordinary and investment accounts there is also a profusion of National Savings 'instruments', perhaps the best known of which are the National Savings Certificates of which there are £3.9 billion in issue. Originally, National Savings Certificates, which were first introduced in 1916, were known as War Savings Certificates. They are 'good as gilts' in terms of security, because the State is directly responsible for payment of interest. The real benefit to the saver from National Savings Certificates has been the high yield. For example, the 14th issue of National Savings Certificates offered the investor a guaranteed interest rate of 7.59 per cent over four years if held for the full four years, and it was a rate which was free of UK income tax at all levels, including the investment income surcharge and capital gains tax. Like the 16th issue, the 14th issue proved so popular as a savings medium, particularly for the surtax payer, that it was the intention to withdraw it in Chancellor Healey's April 1978 Budget, and to replace it from June 1978 by the lower-yielding 17th issue. This intention was overtaken by the general rise in interest rates and the 14th issue was continued, with the maximum individual holding increased to £3,000 from 1 July 1978. However, it is intended that the 17th issue will be introduced when interest rates fall back enough to make it attractive to the investor.

You can see why the 16th issue of National Savings Certificates, which offered a net yield of 8.8 per cent over four years (then equivalent to 13.3 per cent if grossed up to take account of standard rate of tax) was snapped up between mid-December 1976 until certificates were withdrawn, as a result of pressure from the building societies, at the end of March 1977.

But remember that these guaranteed yield Savings Certificates are illiquid so you must hold them for the full four years to reap the benefit. And also bear in mind that the 16th issue was 'end-heavy'; in fact National Savings Certificates always have their interest payments so structured that the holder is penalised for early surrender.

INDEX-LINKED RETIREMENT ISSUES

Index-Linked Retirement Issues are, regrettably, only available to pensioners. This means men of sixty-five and over, and women of sixty plus. Even then, the pensioner cannot have more than £500 worth, although he or she can still hold their entitlement to the 14th issue of National Savings Certificates. The Certificates can be held until the fifth anniversary of purchase and their repayment value is related to the movement of the UK General Index of Retail Prices, so they are inflation-proof. In a period of high inflation – 1974, 1975 and 1976 being record years for inflation – these 'Granny Bonds' are unbeatable value as table 8 shows.

The retirement Certificates must be held for a year to gain the benefits of indexation. Their popularity during high inflation was undoubted, with some £380 million pouring into them. But when high inflation rates started to fall, vividly shown up on table 8, many holders cashed in their certificates and switched their funds to building societies. Normally eight working days' notice is sufficient to secure repayment, and if you want to be cautious and take your profit (a repayment value chart updated monthly is on display at Post Offices), you do not have to cash your total holding to get the index-linked benefit. Just encash sufficient to match the increase in

Table 8. *Index-Linked Retirement Issues*

Date of purchase	Value of £10 certificate at July 1978	Rise %
June 1975	£15.16	+51.6%
September 1975	£14.13	+41.3%
December 1975	£13.73	+37.3%
March 1976	£13.23	+32.3%
June 1976	£12.75	+27.5%
October 1976	£12.35	+23.5%
January 1977	£11.80	+18.0%
April 1977	£11.24	+12.4%
July 1977	£10.77	+7.7%

(At the time of the launch of index-linked retirement certificates in June 1975 the UK Retail Price Index stood at 129.1. At July 1978 the Retail Price Index stood at 195.7)

value of your investment over and above your original capital invested. Bear in mind that the index-linked appreciation is free both of income tax and capital gains tax.

BRITISH SAVINGS BONDS

Around one-third of National Savings Certificates and nearly two-thirds of British Savings Bonds are bought through the clearing banks, which gives some indication that the more sophisticated investors are more aware of their merits than are the savers for whom the National Savings movement is designed. There are £833 million of British Savings Bonds in issue, and the 'Jubilee' issue for example offers a fixed rate of interest of 8½ per cent over a five-year term. The twice-yearly interest payments are subject to tax, but the 'terminal' bonus of 4 per cent is tax free. Interest, by the way, is payable gross of tax. You can hold up to £10,000 of British Savings Bonds (Jubilee Issue). A new issue of bonds, offering 9½%, was launched on 20 November 1978.

PREMIUM BONDS

One of the most popular National Savings schemes, designed to appeal to a nation of gamblers, is the Premium Bond. Its popularity is illustrated by the fact that there are £1,300 million in issue. If you buy one or more you are eligible for inclusion in draws for cash prizes, and the computer 'Ernie' churns out the list of bond winners. When you buy a Premium Bond, you do not get any interest. Instead, the Treasury fixes a rate of interest applicable to the total number of bonds eligible and the resultant interest is payable by way of prize money. The main draw is held at the beginning of each month and there is a subsidiary weekly draw each Saturday.

Each week there is one prize of £75,000 and one of £50,000. Each month there is one prize of £100,000 and one prize of £25,000. Each remaining complete £100,000 of 'interest' payable is divided into one prize of £5,000, ten prizes of £1,000 each, ten prizes of £500 each, twenty-five prizes of £100 each, 1,000 prizes of £50 each and 1,100 £25 prizes. You are not eligible to take part in the draw until you have held your bond, or bonds, for three months. It sounds like a great many prizes, but the chances of a high taxpayer winning enough to make his investment worthwhile are pretty small. The odds of a prize being won by a single bond in each monthly draw are approximately 10,800 to 1. Even with odds like this against you, there are still many prize-winners who do not claim their prizes, and there is a substantial chunk of prize money sitting waiting for prize-winners who are untraceable because they have not notified the Bonds and Stock Office at Lytham St Annes of a change of address or name.

SAVE-AS-YOU-EARN

Save-as-you-earn is the second public-sector, index-linked savings scheme. This is a savings scheme under which for regular monthly payments (a minimum of £4 to a maximum of £20) over a period of five years you get the benefit of index-linking. Over the five years each of your sixty contributions will be separately revalued in line with the movement of the UK General Index of Retail Prices between the month of contribution and the fifth anniversary of the start date of the contract. At the end of five years, if the savings are withdrawn, the sixty revalued contributions will be added together to arrive at the total repayment value, each monthly contribution having been index-linked separately from the first of the month following payment. Alternatively, on completion of the five years the money can be left invested for a further two years. No further contributions are made during these two years. Each of your contributions will then be index-linked in line with the Retail Price Index on the seventh anniversary of the start date of the savings scheme. In addition, a tax-free bonus equal to two monthly contributions is payable. If the monthly payment was £10 then the bonus will be £20. This SAYE scheme is the only regular savings scheme on the market which guarantees the purchasing power of your cash, but it does tie you up for five years to get the benefit of index-linking. Anybody over the age of sixteen can take advantage of the scheme, and you can pay in cash each month over a Post Office counter or by Giro or National Savings Bank standing orders. You get your application forms for the scheme from the Post Office. The index-linked appreciation, by the way, is income tax and capital gains tax free. Bear in mind that Save-As-You-Earn was introduced as recently as 1969 to encourage regular monthly savings in return for an income tax free bonus at the end of a five- or seven-year period. It was only in 1975 that index-linked contracts were introduced into the scheme.

The National Savings movement is a somewhat complex savings area, although designed for those with simple tastes in saving. The very complexity, with the high returns on offer, make some of the opportunities worth exploiting for the sophisticated investor.

Chapter 13

Using the Money Markets

Let us suppose that you have surplus cash to spare, cash which you may need back in a week, a month or in a year's time. If you are inept enough to leave more than a working balance sufficient to avoid bank charges on your current account we have no sympathy for you. Mind you, if you do let your bank keep your spare cash on current account on an interest-free basis you are not alone: a substantial proportion of clearing bank funds are made up of current account balances on which they pay no interest. Let's imagine you are sensible enough to cream off cash surplus to your current account balance and put it on bank deposit. This will earn you a rate of interest but there are a number of normally higher yielding alternatives open to you, alternatives which are flexible enough to enable you to earn a high rate of interest on funds placed for the short-term and for any tailor-made period of up to five years and more.

THE 'WHOLESALE' MONEY MARKETS

Now any money broker worth his salt would say, 'Oh yes, but those more attractive options are quoted for minimum "slabs" of surplus cash of £250,000 or more being dealt in on the City's wholesale money markets.' But what is not generally known is that local authorities (see chapter 10) will take sums as little as £200 because a large volume of small deposits is still attractive to local authorities for their 'advertised' bonds. Local authority negotiable bonds are marketed in amounts of £1,000 plus.

96

The finance houses will also take deposits direct. Discount houses will take deposits in the region of £25,000 and above although they normally deal in much larger amounts. Neither companies nor individuals can deal direct on the inter-bank market, a market in which the average transaction is of the order of £250,000, but your own bank will take 'special' deposits from £10,000 upwards at a small margin under the 'wholesale' money market inter-bank rate of interest. Sterling certificates of deposit are dealt in for minimum amounts of £50,000, while treasury bills, bank bills and trade bills can be bought for £5,000 plus.

MONEY MARKET INSTRUMENTS

Obviously the astute investor has to allow for the unexpected, in which case he may want to realise his surplus cash immediately. This need for liquidity divides the money market into two categories. They are the money market instruments which can be easily bought and sold on an active secondary market – these include sterling certificates of deposit, treasury bills, bank bills, trade bills and, of course, local authority bonds. The second category – deposits with local authorities, finance houses, discount houses and special deposits with your bank – involves waiting until maturity to collect your deposit plus interest. However, even if your funds were locked up in this way until maturity and, in the interim, you suddenly found yourself strapped for cash, it is improbable that your bank would refuse to advance you temporary funds if you waved a deposit receipt in front of the manager – although you would then be paying a rate of interest on your borrowed funds which has to be offset against the rate of interest you are earning on your deposit.

MECHANICS OF THE MARKET PLACE

What about costs? If you have enough confidence to feel that you can get the best for yourself then you can deal direct and incur no costs, but this method of operation does mean that you have to monitor constantly the changing spectrum of interest rates available on the money markets.

One point to bear in mind, though, is that if you want to shop around for the best rate of interest available you really need a bank account at a bank (or bank branch) within the City's Square Mile. This means you can switch your funds without any loss of interest while surplus cash is being transferred from one City branch to another under the 'Town' clearing system. All over the City's Square Mile at about mid-afternoon you can see messengers scurrying breathlessly from one bank to another with sheaves of cheques in order to secure a 'value today' basis for money market transactions. The alternative is the 'general' clearing system through which the bulk (in terms of number – not value) of our cheques are cleared, but this system involves some delay, and delay costs money in terms of loss of interest.

You can, of course, use a money broker whose job it is to guide those with cash to spare to the highest yielding home and borrowers from the money markets to the cheapest source of finance. If you walked into a money broker's dealing room you would get a first, frenetic impression made up from a mêlée of winking lights from the serried ranks of telephone panels signalling the ebb and flow of millions of pounds and foreign currencies around the markets, together with a hubbub of bawled instructions. There are over two dozen money brokers established in and around the City in places such as St Swithin's Lane, New and Old Broad Streets, Chiswell Street and Ludgate Hill.

The broker may seem to earn a good commission for only a couple of phone calls, but bear in mind that he is working in a very tightly integrated market in which the quotation of a rate of interest which is minutely out of line means that the broker will probably lose the deal, and with it his commission and something also of his firm's reputation. In addition the brokers have to pay high rents, high salaries and have to instal a lot of very expensive telecommunications equipment, plus putting in, at their own expense, direct lines to many of their most important customers.

INVESTMENT THROUGH THE MONEY FUNDS

At present there are only two true money funds in existence.

They are the Simco Three-Month Fund and the Simco Seven-Day Fund. Simco stands for the Saturn Investment Management Company which in turn is a subsidiary of the leading City-based money-broking group, M.W. Marshall (20 Cannon Street, London EC4M 6XD). The idea of the funds is simple enough: to pool together many small deposits in order to gain access to the much higher interest rates offered for bigger chunks of cash by the clearing banks and local authorities.

The Simco Seven-Day Fund: This fund is for depositors who do not want to tie their cash up for longer than seven days, and the fund is open to depositors having a minimum amount of £1,000. Additional deposits, and withdrawals, must be for less than £500. The interest on your deposit is calculated as follows: the total amount of interest earned by the fund every day is divided by the total amount deposited to arrive at the 'daily average rate'. This is the interest rate your money actually earns, and interest is earned by a depositor from the time his cheque is cleared until the day before the money is paid out. Interest is paid half-yearly on 31 March and 30 September or on the total repayment of your deposit. One point to bear in mind is that interest is paid gross, without deduction of income tax, so you have the added sweetener of earning interest on your tax liability (depending on your rate of tax) until the Revenue actually collects.

The Simco Three-Month Fund: This fund works in exactly the same way except that depositors place their money in the fund for three months. Normally the rate of interest obtainable on three-month money from the inter-bank or local authorities markets is higher than it is for seven-day deposits. The money deposited earns interest at the agreed rate throughout the three-month period and then receives repayment automatically on the seventh day following the end of the three months (called 'the repayment day') – unless, of course, the investor tells Saturn that he wants his money rolled over for a further three-month period or transferred to the Seven-day Fund.

Now if you happen to have money hanging around spare on a day other than the weekly subscription day (every Wednesday), then Saturn have thought about this too, and have created the Simco Subscription Account pending investment on the following Wednesday. During this period the depositor gets paid the 'call money rate', so his deposits are never sitting idle. Similarly, at the end of a fixed period, when his funds mature (and maybe he thinks money market rates are going to rise over the next week or fortnight so he does not want to lock away his funds for three months before the interest rates are jacked up), he can leave his money sitting on the Subscription Account until he decides to push it back into the three-month fund.

Management Charges: As with unit trusts or commodity trusts, there are management charges to be taken into consideration. Saturn charges a management fee of ⅜ per cent per annum of the capital sum deposited and deducts this from the accumulated interest due to the depositor on repayment, or on renewal of the deposit. And if you want to route your deposit through your stockbroker, accountant, solicitor or bank manager (in return for a quid pro quo such as reduced accountancy fees or bank charges) then Saturn pay a return commission of .06 per cent to agents.

Mechanics are simple enough. If you are interested enough you merely telephone Saturn and ask what rate is being quoted for the three-month or the seven-day fund. If you like the sound of it then you tell the dealers how much you want to deposit and send a cheque either to the National Westminster Bank, 27 Cannon Street, London EC4M 5SA for the credit of Simco Three-Month Account or, in the case of the seven-day fund, the Simco Capital Account, or direct to Saturn. To avoid lost interest while your cheque is in process of transmission, do not forget to tell your bank to use the telegraphic transfer system for amounts over £5,000. A couple of days of lost interest could mean a couple of bottles (or even crates) of whisky to you.

A word about security, something we are all keen on knowing about since the financial traumas of 1973 and 1974. Saturn restricts its investment only to UK local authorities (which has the Government-backed Public Works Loan Board standing behind them) or to the clearing banks (Barclays, Midland, Lloyds, National Westminster etc.) and their wholly-owned subsidiaries. The money is lent out for periods which exactly match that of the original deposit period, so there is maximum safety allied with total liquidity. Saturn does not go in for 'taking positions' with other people's money. Saturn itself acts only on a special trustee basis as manager of the funds; it does not become the 'beneficial' owner of any of the funds deposited – and an audit is carried out by an independent firm of accountants monthly on the three-month fund and weekly on the seven-day fund.

OTHER OPTIONS OPEN

There are two other routes for the smaller investor to gain access to the wholesale money market rates. One is to deal through either Williams & Glyn's or Midland Bank in Jersey, both of whom are prepared to quote a rate of interest approaching the wholesale rate for deposits over £3,000.

The second is to place money on deposit with United Dominions Trust (5 Eastcheap, EC3 or any branch) which offers ½ per cent over the average of the preceding week's local authority deposit rate, for deposits of £1,000 and over for maturities of seven days and more.

Chapter 14

Successful Investment in Commodities

A century or so ago suppliers sold commodities – silver, zinc, lead, tin, copper, cocoa, sugar, coffee, rubber, soya beans, grain – to manufacturing companies in the normal way of business. Today, the underlying purpose of commodity trading remains exactly the same, with the raw commodities being processed and ultimately used or consumed. Commodity investment came into the picture about a hundred years ago when a market developed in which people who had nothing to do with physical commodity trading, but who had cash to spare, could invest in order to make a capital gain. This injection of outside cash meant that the commodity traders were freed from the need to lock up cash in commodity stocks, as the cash of the investors became the lubricant which enabled the commodity markets to expand at a faster rate during a period of a massive increase in both the consuming population and in manufacturing industry. The commodity future markets, through which commodity future contracts are bought and sold (and the existence of a future contract means that it can be bought and sold in the market and the investor need never take physical delivery), evolved naturally out of this basic need.

An investor can buy or sell forward for periods of up to twenty-four months in advance for a down payment, normally, of only a 10 per cent 'security deposit' (more on the subject of this 'gearing' element later). There is no stamp duty to pay, and commissions to brokers should be around ½ per cent of the total contract value. Unlike shares, there are relatively few commodities to monitor, the 'hard' commodities and the 'soft'

102

commodities. A list of the main dealing commodities, the normal contract sizes and the price/weight in which they are expressed is shown below.

Commodity	*Normal Contract Sizes*	*Price/Weight*
Copper	25 tons	£ per ton
Tin	5 tons	£ per ton
Lead	25 tons	£ per ton
Zinc	25 tons	£ per ton
Silver	10,000 ozs.	Pence per troy ounce
Cocoa	20 tons	£ per ton
Sugar	50 tons	£ per ton
Coffee	5 tons	£ per ton
Rubber	15 tons	Pence per kilo
Soya Beans	100 tons	£ per ton
Grains	100 tons	£ per ton

DEALING DIRECT

If you want to deal direct in commodities you have the choice of handing your capital – usually £5,000 and upwards – over to a commodity dealer or trading on your own behalf, but putting your deals through a broker. The strategy of handing your cash over to be managed for you by an expert (sometimes called a 'discretionary account') has the advantage that you do not have to make the decisions yourself, so you are relieved of that particular responsibility. Discretionary accounts are less risky also because, as the commodity broker takes the dealing decisions for you and will not want to lose a client, he will probably pursue a fairly conservative investment policy on your behalf. The other advantage is that you have 'limited liability' in the sense that you cannot lose more than the original amount of the capital you hand over. The broker will send you a monthly statement of your account, and you will be charged his brokerage commission, so it is worth ringing round a few brokers to ask for a list of their brokerage charges.

The Trading Account: The more risky trading account means that you have to monitor the commodity markets yourself, make your own decisions when to buy and sell and the broker collects a straightforward brokerage charge. When you complete a client's agreement form for a trading account, the broker will check out your credit standing to establish what you are good for. That is because you can take advantage of the 'gearing' effect available on the commodities futures market, which means that you normally have to put down only 10 per cent of the face value of the future contract so your capital has ten times its buying power. This enables you to take up a relatively large number of 'positions' in commodities on a limited amount of capital. But you will have to be prepared to make available additional cash so that you can top up your margins when the market goes against you. The doctrine of unlimited liability prevails in direct dealing of this type and you, the client, bear all the risks: and you indemnify the broker in the event of default on your account.

COMMODITY TRADERS' TERMS: WHAT THEY MEAN

Commodity Options: Instead of buying a commodity contract you can purchase a commodity option which limits your risk if there is no definite price trend in the market, but at the cost of paying a premium. The option can be taken up or abandoned, depending on whether the commodity price moves in the right direction or the wrong direction.

Call Option: A call option gives you the right to buy at an agreed price any time between the day you buy the option and the date it expires. It is a suitable tactic to use if you think the market will rise.

Put Option: A put option gives you the right to sell at an agreed price any time between the day you buy the option and the date it expires. It is a suitable tactic to use when you think the market will go down.

Double Option: This works both ways (not, however, at the same time), but you have to pay twice the call or put option premiums.

Declaration Date: The date by which all options must be exercised or abandoned.

Premium: The premium is determined by market volatility, the current and anticipated price level of the particular commodity, the level of option demand, and the length of option time granted.

Straddling: This means speculating on the price differentials between different delivery months for commodities. If the investor is sure that differentials in future prices for a particular commodity are out of line he places a straddle by buying for the (in his judgement) under-priced month and simultaneously selling the same amount for delivery in the month he judges to be over-priced.

ABOUT THE PREMIUM

Generally speaking, the premium which you pay for an option is determined by the length of time the option has to run and the state of the market at the time you are buying. Normally the premium will be higher the longer the period of the option and the more volatile the market.

As a rough guide, the premium will normally be in the range of 5 per cent to 15 per cent of the market value of the contract. The premium for a double option, as you might expect, is about twice the premium paid for a put or call option. It is quoted in pounds per ton or in pence per ounce.

For example, the cost of an option over 50 tons of sugar, if the premium is £6, is £600. If the price of sugar rises enough during the period of the option to provide you with a capital gain over and above the cost of the option, then it is worth exercising the option and taking your profit. If it does not, then you should allow your option to lapse – and lose your £600.

KEEPING YOUR EYE ON THE BALL

In commodity speculation the first things to watch out for are major price trends. The problem is that it is difficult to spot when a trend is at the beginning, middle, or end of its course. If you can establish your position in the direction of a major trend and you can keep that position through one-third of the movement, then you should reap good profits. But risk only a small amount of your trading capital in any one deal: you cannot afford to have a position counter to a major trend and to hold it for any length of time because you would absorb all your trading capital. So cut your losses and let your profits run.

Use stop orders to limit your exposure to a big loss. A stop order becomes a market order when the stop price, which can be fixed above or below the market price at which you buy, is reached.

TAXATION

The Inland Revenue's treatment of gains from commodity trading is something of a grey area (truth to tell, the taxation map has more grey-shaded areas than black or white). There are no firm rulings on whether gains should be liable to capital gains tax or to the bigger burden of income tax. Decisions vary between tax districts and also between individual cases. In practice, commodity traders have found that buyers of physical commodities frequently manage to get gains assessed under capital gains tax. It helps the case to have held the commodity for a year or more. Capital gains on commodity futures are more likely to be taxed as income, particularly if the speculative nature of the operation is reinforced by borrowings with which to finance the deals. Funds placed under professional management can usually be categorised as a capital gain and taxed as such.

Chapter 15

Successful Investment in Commodity Funds

If you are thinking of investing in commodities use only the last 10 to 15 per cent of your free capital. In the last analysis, it has to be that bit of your capital which you can afford to lose if the market – and the commodity market is notoriously volatile – turns against you. While rises in commodities can be spectacular, as in 1976, experience shows that no one investment sector goes on rising for ever and booms inevitably become slumps as sure as night follows day. Remember that back in 1974 copper prices fell over a precipice and plummeted from £1,400 to under £600 per ton. And you also have to allow for things no investment expert or commodity broker can predict – earthquakes, frosts, storms and vagaries of domestic and international politics, all of which can have a dramatic effect on the prices of particular commodities. Bear in mind also, along with the fact that the only certainty about commodity prices is that they are unpredictable, that commodities yield no income – only the chance of a capital gain or loss.

COMMODITY FUNDS

Commodity funds, the least risky end of commodity investment, are for those having from £300 to £5,000 to spare, and they are run on the lines of a unit trust. There are two types of commodity fund. The first is the commodity-based fund, akin to a unit trust, which offers the investor an indirect route into commodity investment as the funds do not invest directly in commodities themselves but instead invest in the shares of companies which are linked to the commodity markets either because they produce commodities, or directly trade in them. Ebor Commodity Fund is probably the best known, while Rothschild's and Save & Prosper are also in this field. For advice about these funds talk to your stockbroker, or if you have not got a stockbroker ask your bank manager to obtain, through his investment department, advice from one of the brokers who specialise in these funds. These funds are the lowest-risk way of investing in commodities, but bear in mind also that the rewards are unlikely to be spectacular either. Also, of course, there is some income flow from your investment as the funds invest in companies, and companies pay dividends so long as they are making a profit.

OFF-SHORE FUNDS

A higher-risk, but more direct, route, is to invest in commodity funds based in the Channel Islands or the Isle of Man (hence the term 'off-shore'). They are located in these off-shore tax havens primarily for tax benefit reasons and the funds are operated on unit trust lines, which means that shares in the trusts can be bought and sold at any time. Most of the funds appoint a subsidiary of a UK clearing bank as a trustee, but too much should not be made of this since a trustee tends to operate as a custodian rather than as a watchdog over the commodity funds. The other point to bear in mind about these funds is that they are 'unauthorised' by the Department of Trade and therefore are forbidden to promote themselves by means such as advertising. The funds invest in a wide spread of commodities in the same way as unit trusts invest in a wide spread of equities on the UK and overseas stock markets. Shares in commodity funds can be bought either through your stockbroker or through your bank.

Commodity funds of this type can be separately categorised as to whether they follow a low-risk investment policy, a high-risk investment policy or a middle-of-the-road path. A low-risk commodity fund would follow a policy of restricting its risk by buying and holding commodities such as copper or silver as long-term investments, and would not get involved in the higher risk areas of gearing, future contracts and options.

Low-Risk Versus High-Risk: Examples of low-risk off-shore commodity funds are provided by the Silver Trust or Copper Trust which are run by Surinvest. They follow a policy of buying and holding copper and silver for the long term and hoping ultimately to sell at profit. The investor can put aside £500 and upwards in one of these funds and it is a way of putting your capital into inflation hedges such as copper and silver without all the trouble of doing so yourself: if you buy silver direct, for example, which UK residents are allowed to hold, then you do attract VAT if you take physical delivery of the metal, and you have all the headaches of storage and insurance.

At the other end of the risk scale, Chart Analysis, through its offshoot Commodity Analysis, runs a Commodities and Options fund which engages in the full gamut of speculative commodity transactions with the one restriction that 30 to 50 per cent of the fund's assets are kept on deposit.

'Middle-of-the-Road' Funds: Two major middle-of-the-road funds are the Old Court Commodity Fund (run by Rothschild's through Old Court Commodity Fund Managers) and the Save and Prosper (Jersey) Commodity Fund. The policy of the latter is to invest in commodities and the fund is also allowed to buy futures as long as at least 66 per cent of the commodity contract is kept on deposit. The great danger area for commodity speculators – uncovered forward sales (contracting to sell something you have not got) – is avoided and there are also rules about the extent of the use of put and call options. Other middle-of-the-road funds spread their risk vulnerability by investing in commodities, by using most of the sophisticated commodity speculation techniques, and by investing in commodity shares which are less risky. First Viking Trust, which is advised by commodity brokers M.L. Doxford, comes into this category, as does the Rothschild's Old Court Fund.

COMMODITY SYNDICATES

Lastly, a number of commodity brokers run commodity syndicates on an unofficial basis for some of their smaller clients, rather like the merchant bankers who shovel the small fry clientele into an in-house unit trust because the profitability from dealing with small accounts is non-existent and it is easier to pool them.

By the way, do not be put off by the fact that funds investing directly in commodities are located off-shore, a soubriquet which has something of the colour of IOS to it. The funds are located in Britain's off-shore islands – Jersey, Guernsey and the Isle of Man – because of existing UK laws which prohibit the advertising and promotion of commodity syndicates and also because of the tax advantages of these islands. But bear in mind that finance centres such as St Helier are not in the same category as the Cayman Islands. The islanders police their banks and other financial institutions pretty vigorously, and the banks themselves are subject to the strictures of the Bank of England.

TIPS ON COMMODITY FUNDS

First, bear in mind that these off-shore commodity funds, and the on-shore commodity funds which invest in commodity related companies, are 'open-ended', so you can buy and sell your shares in the funds at any time.

Second, always check the charging system of the fund management company. The system whereby the managers' reward for their services is geared to the financial heft of the big investors can work to the disadvantage of the small investor, so read the small print.

Third, bear in mind that the commodity investment market – even by way of commodity funds – is no different from any other investment market. Success is all a matter of timing and capital gains come from getting in somewhere near the bottom and out near the top. Not many of us can do this, but be content with a reasonable gain and take your profits. Do not be greedy and hang on until your particular commodity boom is pricked and you watch your uncashed profits disappear like snow in the Sahara.

Lastly, choose a fund whose investment policy best suits your needs. If you can afford to gamble, and maybe lose most of the cash you have set aside for commodity investment, then go for the high-risk fund. If you cannot then go for the middle-of-the-road fund. And if you want the chance of reasonable capital gain, plus some income, then choose an on-shore commodity fund which invests in companies linked to the commodity markets.

Chapter 16

Successful Investment in Gold Coins

Despite determined efforts by individual governments and by international monetary authorities to 'de-monetise' gold and so remove it from the investment scene, the lesson of all recorded history is that they are unlikely to be successful. Apart from the fact that the yellow metal is attractive to look at and feels good to handle, its continuing lure is provided by the fact that no satisfactory substitute has been found for it, that it is acceptable as a store of value and medium of exchange throughout the world, and that (unlike silver) it is fundamentally linked to the world's monetary system despite all protestations that such a link between 'hard currencies' and a lifeless metal is a nonsense. Then again, the effects of two world wars, of economic depressions and of spiralling inflation have created great suspicion as to the worth of holding paper currency. The French, for example, have always been suspicious of notes produced by the Government printing presses and have a built-in preference for gold 'Napoleons'. Even the British witnessed an astonishing change of sentiment as recently as 1974 – astonishing in that the British are not noted gold-coin holders, but the traumas of 1974 triggered off a massive rush into krugerrands and sovereigns as a hedging operation against the advent of the seemingly imminent apocalypse. So great was the rush into gold coins that Chancellor Healey clamped down on both gold coin imports and on the domestic manufacture of sovereigns.

   As you can readily see, gold is so attractive that governments have to control the conditions under which their residents are allowed to buy it. In Britain we are not allowed to buy gold

Table 9. *Bullion Gold Coins*

Coin	*Country of origin*
Krugerrand	South Africa
King Edward Sovereigns	UK
Queen Elizabeth Sovereigns	UK
100 Corona	Austria
50 pesos	Mexico
Double Eagle	USA
Single Eagle	USA
Half Eagle	USA
20 Francs (Napoleon)	France
20 Francs	Switzerland
20 Marks	Germany
20 Francs	Belgium
20 Lire	Italy

in bar form, yet 'standard gold bars' account for the vast bulk of the world's trade in gold. The British are, however, allowed to buy gold coins, which can be loosely divided into two sectors. One sector is 'bullion' gold coins. These are coins, listed in table 9, whose value is primarily determined by their gold content and whose prices always reflect a premium over and above the price of the intrinsic gold contained by the coin.

The other sector of gold coins comprises the 'numismatic' gold coins. The value of these coins is determined not so much by their gold content as by their rarity – so that the prices they command on the market bear little relation to the weight of gold they contain. These include gold coins such as the Gold Solidus of the Emperor Heraclius Constantine (613–630 AD) or the USA $10 'Liberty Head' of 1799. This chapter concentrates solely on bullion gold coins, although chapter 17 will investigate the investment merits of the numismatic gold coin market.

GOLD COINS – BACKGROUND

To understand the investment merits and demerits of bullion gold coins it is necessary to appreciate the background to gold in the last seventy years, because it is fundamentally upon the price of gold that the price of bullion gold coins depends.

During the nineteenth century, note issues by commercial banks became increasingly rare and central banks – in the case of the UK, the Bank of England – took over a steadily increasing share of this responsibility. Paper currency like pound notes was, as it had always been, freely convertible into gold and was (fractionally) backed by gold, hence the 'gold standard'. Between the two world wars virtually all countries of the world abandoned the gold standard, with the result that currency was no longer convertible into gold. In August 1914 the gold standard was suspended, never to be fully restored, although in 1925 a modified gold standard known as the 'gold bullion standard' (so called because gold coins were no longer in circulation) was re-introduced and lasted, with somewhat disastrous results for employment, until 1931. The gold market in London – upon which newly mined gold and other gold is sold to the highest bidder every working day – was closed at the start of World War II and was re-opened in 1954. The price of gold was kept by the monetary authorities within the narrow range of $35 per ounce: this price was the 'monetary' level ('monetary' gold being gold stocks held by central banks as part of their individual country's central reserves), the price it had been in 1934. This lasted until 1960 when uncertainty about the US dollar led to heavy demand for gold and a consequent upsurge in its price to over $40. This in turn led to the formation of the International Gold Pool, a consortium of leading central banks, whose market operations limited the gold price to around $35 for eight years. By 1968 demand for gold had become so heavy that the Pool withdrew from the market and agreement was reached that monetary gold should be segregated from free-market gold.

This marked the beginning of the two-tier gold market system. Monetary gold was fixed at $35 an ounce and free-market gold left to find its own price level. The price of monetary gold was raised to $38 an ounce in 1971, and then to $42.22 in 1973. The price of free-market gold reached a peak on 30 December 1974 – at $197½ per ounce. Since that peak was reached during the gloom and despond of the winter of 1974 when inflation was raging throughout the industrialised world, when the UK Stock Market was within a few points of 146 (as recorded by the *Financial Times* 30-share index), and when otherwise sane and sensible City financiers were talking about the merits of a stock of canned food with which to survive the imminent collapse – gold fell back to bottom out at $103 per ounce in the summer of 1976 due to the return of confidence that the Western industrial structure was not about to collapse and that other forms of income-yielding investments such as shares and gilts could once again be trusted, and due also to the successive IMF gold auctions designed to de-monetise gold. Since the $103 price was reached – at which point City investment experts were writing off gold and by implication gold coins as an investment completely – the price of gold has staged the inevitable come-back.

UK RESIDENTS AND GOLD COINS

Until April 1971 the 'Rule of Four' prevailed so far as gold coins were concerned. Under the Rule of Four it was not possible for UK residents to buy gold coins without the specific consent of the Bank of England, and even when this consent was granted they were limited to a prescribed number – four – of each specimen. Shortly after this restriction was lifted came a time (1973–4) when the gold price was steadily soaring and when gold coins looked a pretty effective way of insulating part at least of one's capital against the eroding effects of inflation. Coin dealers mushroomed overnight. One clearing bank records an individual walking into one of its Sheffield branches and placing a single order of £250,000 for kruger-rands. The flood of British capital into gold coins, particularly South African krugerrands (a gold coin which is roughly the size of the old half-crown and weighs slightly more than a Troy ounce due to the slight additional weight of the alloy), caused Healey to clamp down in his April 1975 Budget. 'The time has come,' he announced to the House of Commons, 'to stop this drain' (the cost in foreign exchange of gold coins coming in from abroad) 'which has amounted to on average £25 million a month in the first quarter of this year.'

The net result of the Healey measures was to bar gold coin imports by UK residents. The position since April 1975 is that authorised banks and dealers in gold can import post-1837 (later changed to post-1937) gold coins only if they are

115

intended for re-export or for sale to other authorised dealers. The UK has about 100 authorised dealers, including the clearing banks, who had to apply for licences under the new rules. At the same time the Bank of England announced an end to new sovereign sales to UK residents. This created a two-tier market in gold coins in the UK, the domestic market and the international market. The domestic market is constituted by a pool of coins – principally krugerrands and sovereigns – which were bought by UK residents before the stable door was firmly bolted. The pool is static, as it cannot be added to by imports or by the minting of new, UK-produced sovereigns. The only coins available for sale are those which are made available by other UK residents. Initially the price of krugerrands and sovereigns jumped – by £8 a coin for krugerrands. Inevitably, though, due to the publicity given by the press during the boom buying days of 1973 and 1974 there are still plenty of krugerrands left in the domestic pool, and there are still a good supply of sovereigns. However, British investors in bullion gold coins never took to the lesser known coins such as the Mexican 50-pesos piece (despite the fact that its premium at that time was less than the premium on krugerrands), or the Austrian 100-Corona or the French, German, Swiss, Belgian or Italian gold coins. The small number of these latter coins held in Britain means that the market in them dried up after the Healey measures.

A 'spread' is quoted for each coin (eg. £101–£102 for a krugerrand) and this spread represents the dealer's profits because he sells at the higher of the two prices quoted and is prepared to buy back at the lower of the two prices. For you to break even, the price of the coin has to move up by at least the amount of the spread.

PREMIUMS AND TAXATION

The premium attached to a gold coin, which may be as low as 3 per cent or may top the 20 per cent mark – is made up by both the extra amount the investor pays for the coin's intrinsic gold metal content over and above what he would pay for the same amount of gold in a non-coin form and also by supply and demand conditions in the market prevailing at the time of purchase or sale. The effect of the premium on the price of a King Edward sovereign is shown in the following example.

Let us suppose that the gold price is $180 per ounce and its sterling equivalent is £96.26 per ounce. A King Edward sovereign contains 0.2354oz of fine gold. The worth of this gold is 0.2354 × £96.26 = £22.66, but the buyer's price could be £31.56 for the coin, in which case the buyer is paying a fairly substantial premium of almost 40 per cent.

To take the example of the krugerrand, this coin is made of standard gold, that is to say 22-carat gold with a standard fineness of 11/12ths fine gold and 1/12th alloy. The standard weight of the coin is 33.93107 grams, or slightly more than a troy ounce, which weighs 32.50 grams, the additional weight being that of the alloy. With the price of gold being £96.26 and the buyer's price of a krugerrand being £99¼, the buyer is paying a premium that is very little over the odds (3 per cent) for a coin which consists of an ounce of gold of a fineness of .9166 (the fineness of gold bars ranges from .995, the minimum gold content accepted in a bar, to .9999, which is virtually pure gold).

Gold coins are graded as to quality (see page 120), and the slightest change in the condition of a coin can reduce its market value. This is why investment krugerrands, for example, are sold in plastic cases.

As far as investment is concerned, bear in mind that there is only the opportunity of capital gain or loss. Gold coins yield no income and there are the costs of insurance and storage to take into account if you choose to keep them in a bank.

Capital gains tax is chargeable (or capital losses are off-settable) on all forms of coin gains from re-sale, with the exception of sovereigns. Sovereigns, being still officially coin of the realm, are not subject to capital gains tax.

BEWARE OF SMALL DEALERS

If you are wise you will deal direct with one of the five members of the London Gold Market – Johnson, Matthey; Mocatta and Goldsmid; Samuel Montagu; N.M. Rothschild; and Sharps, Pixley – rather than with a coin dealer. The main reason for so doing is that the coin dealer has to buy from one of the five members of the Gold Market himself in the first place and therefore adds on his 'turn'. Secondly, the lessons of 1974 and 1975 have shown that coin dealers who mushroom overnight when there is euphoria in the gold coin market are not necessarily around when you want to sell the coins you have bought. Normally the five members of the London Gold Market deal for orders of ten coins and above, but Johnson, Matthey will deal with smaller orders. Your clearing bank will also buy coins on your behalf – for a small commission – as will a stockbroker.

Johnson Matthey
5 Lloyds Ave., EC3   Head Office
01-481-3181   01-882-6111

Chapter 17

Successful Investment in Collectors' Coins

THE UNDERPINNING TO THE COIN MARKET

There are four main reasons why the collectors' coin market has developed from the era when it was the somewhat esoteric preserve of university professors, who used coins as significant historical guideposts tracing the way into vanished ages, into the fast-booming investment market of the late 1950s, 1960s and (with a hiccup in 1974) the 1970s.

The first is that the market is heavily underpinned by the large number of collectors as opposed to investors. The second is that coins are small and easily portable and so present an excellent opportunity for those who wish to transfer some or all of their wealth across frontiers. The third is that coins, judged by the history of price movements in the market since the late 1950s, offer an excellent hedge against both currency fluctuations and against the ravages of inflation which can so easily burn up the real worth of paper assets. The fourth is that coins offer the high taxpayer the opportunity for capital gain.

The strength of collectors' support to the market can easily be seen as one studies the packed columns of the *Numismatic Circular*, published monthly by Spink and Son Ltd, 5, 6 and 7 King Street, St James's, London SW1 (01-930 7888). Thus '9012 Crete, Gortyna (c. 300 BC) Slater 169.9 grs. Naked Europa seated in willow tree with swan between thighs. R. Bull standing to right looking back licking flank. F/V.F £430' appears in the Greek series. '9171 Ancient British. Gallo Belgic

119

A. Ambiana Slater. With head and horse facing right. Weight 7.70 gms. Struck on a small flan, very rare. Good V.F. £12,000', is taken from the British series.

From an investment point of view, the existence of a solid underpinning to the coin market in the form of collectors, who pore lovingly over details such as these two examples (taken from many hundreds), is important because the market is given stability. True collectors are interested in the coins as coins – the price they can fetch on the open market is a by-product. This means that a decline in coin price levels, like that which took place in 1975, does not turn into a stampede when all coin collectors and investors try to unload their holdings at the same time. Unlike the stock market, collectors will generally tend to hang on through thick and thin in price-level terms. True, price levels did go down from their 1974 peaks – when a five-guinea gold piece fetched £26,000 at a Douglas Morris sale – in 1975, but this was due to the subsidence of speculative froth in the market and to some forced selling triggered off by the collapse of property, gilt and share markets.

However, the importance of collectors in the market means that the investor has to become something of an expert, or get expert advice, on numismatic coins to ensure that he is paying the right price for the right coin and is not being taken in by fakes.

COIN GRADING

The condition of a coin (its 'grading') is all important. The slightest change in the condition of a coin or its patina or the portrait it carries can greatly reduce its price. Cleaning a coin is not acceptable, and it will not fox the experts.

Coins are graded as follows:

FDC   Fleur de coin, mint state.
BU   Brilliant, uncirculated. This is a coin in pristine condition, in as good condition as when it left the Mint.
Unc.   Uncirculated.
EF   Extremely fine.

VF   Very fine. The coin has had no dents to its edge. Some wear on the high points of the design is permissible, but the coin should have no scratches on the 'field' round the design.

F   Fine. The lowest acceptable grade unless the coin is very rare or extremely old.

It is possible to get combinations of gradings, but only two at a time. 'VF-EF' denotes a coin whose general condition is between 'very fine' and 'extremely fine'. 'F/VF' means that one side of the coin (the obverse) is in 'fine' condition while the other side (the reverse) is 'very fine'. It is easy for the non-expert to end up paying a 'very fine' price for only a 'fine' (or worse) coin.

Robin Blackmore, the numismatic coin expert, provides five rules for the investor contemplating buying coins.

Rule 1. Buy only from a reputable dealer who is a member of either the International Association of Professional Numismatists or the British Numismatic Trade Association, or who can offer an unconditional guarantee that the coins you will buy from him are genuine and accurately graded.

Rule 2. Buy only coins in the best condition that is available, but since it may not always be possible to find pieces in Extremely Fine condition, for example, do be realistic.

Rule 3. Do not make the mistake of thinking that you only need to buy any coin in good condition. You also need to know the coin's potential and its future saleability. This is where expert knowledge or advice is needed.

Rule 4. Coin collecting, as you will already have gathered, is a complex business. Make sure you study sale catalogues and dealers' lists, and compare different dealers' prices for the same coins.

Rule 5. Watch that grading – it is the most important element in the price you get for your coin.

THE COIN MARKET – BACKGROUND

In the late 1950s and early 1960s coin prices started to move ahead quickly as buyers recognised their investment potential and as some of the more 'traditional' investment sectors waned in attractions. Prices hit a peak in 1974 and then came the inevitable shake-out in 1975. In 1976 coin prices started to increase again, particularly in the stronger economies of the US, West Germany and France, but also in the UK as investors sought to diversify their portfolio into sectors which offered some protection against both banana republic levels of inflation, and the ever-sinking pound. Have coins proved a good investment over a sustained period of years? Stanley Gibbons' coin expert reckons that if an investor had put £100 into the coin market before 1950, buying a selection of Greek, Roman and British medieval coins, that collection would have increased in value to £10,000. So a coin investment would have outperformed nearly every investment sector and would have beaten a representative selection of blue-chip ordinary shares bought at the same time into a cocked hat. However, it is worth bearing in mind that such a coin investor would have been lucky, in that he would have entered the coin market before it was even considered an investment sector – such powers of foresight belong, alas, to few of us. Table 10 provides more concrete evidence of coin price movements for both gold and silver coins.

CONCENTRATING ON A SECTOR

The coin collectors' market is a vast one and it is worth concentrating on becoming something of an expert in one sector, say English coins. For example English coins can themselves be sub-divided into 'hammered' gold coins (and silver coins) and 'milled' gold and silver coins. Hammered coins lack the milled serrations around the circumference. Many of the famous English denominations can be found in the hammered series such as the angel, noble, sovereign, crown etc. Many of these have increased in price by over 50 per cent each year in recent years. Robin Blackmore reckons that coins in this sector in Extremely Fine condition are still worth buying at the right price, but he does not recommend Fine condition hammered gold coins as he reckons they have peaked out and demand has fallen away. For example, an Edward III noble ('Treaty series. Calais mint. Saltfire before ED and C in the

Table 10. *Numismatic Gold Coin Price Movements*
1965–75*

	1965	1975
USA Liberty Head Gold $10 dated 1799	£400	£1,000
Spain, Ferdinand and Isabella (1476–1516) Gold 2 Excellentes of Seville	£55	£650
Spain, Peter I (1350-1369) Gold Dobla	£75	£1,000
Byzantine Emperor Heraclius and his son Heraclius Constantine (AD 613-630) Gold Solidus	£30	£240
Roman Emperor Commodus (AD 177-192) Gold Aureus struck at Rome	£375	£7,000
William III (1694-1702) Proof Silver Half-Crown	£300	£900
Scotland, Mary Stuart (1542-67) Silver Testoon dated 1562	£350	£2,000
Italy, Naples, Joachim Murat (1808-1815) Silver 5 Lire dated 1813	£30	£250
India, Bombay, Charles II (1660-1685) Silver Rupee of 1678	£75	£600
Henry VIII (1509-1547) Silver Half Groat of Canterbury	£4	£35
Italy, Ferrara, Hercules D'Este (1471-1505) Silver Grossone	£37	£150
Offa King of Mercia (757-796) Silver Penny, Moneyer Alhumun	£850	£2,500
King Alexander the Great of Macedon (336-323 BC) Silver Tetradrachm struck at Babylon	£75	£400
Sicily, King Agathokles (317-289 BC) Silver Tetradrachm	£675	£6,000
Northern Greece, struck at Olynthos under the Chalkidian league (355-352 BC) Silver Tetradrachm	£350	£4,900

(* Coin prices supplied by Spink & Son Ltd)

centre of reverse. Struck from rusty dies, full') would cost you over £1,000 for an Extremely Fine specimen.

Milled gold coins are the most popular coins as far as English collectors are concerned, and five-guinea, two-guinea and guinea coins have proved good investments. Again, Robin Blackmore reckons that prices have risen too high too quickly, and recommends going only for guineas, half-guineas, Victorian sovereigns and half-sovereigns in Very Fine condition or better. As an example, a George II proof guinea of 1729 ('Later young head. Reverse with square shield. Struck a little off centre but very rare') in Extremely Fine condition would cost you around £2,200.

Hammered silver coins (silver penny, groats, testoons) start with the small sceats from the Anglo-Saxon period and run through to the coins of Charles II. There is a lot of potential in this sector: an Edward III groat (1327-77) in Very Fine condition would cost around £60, while a penny from the same reign would cost £35.

Milled silver coins start with Charles II, and prices in this sector are lower than they should be so this could be a good time to buy. A George I 1720 milled silver coin in Extremely Fine condition would cost you around £650.

Blackmore also reckons that copper and bronze coins could be a very good investment over a seven to eight-year period, and this is the least expensive sector in which to start as £1,000 outlay would buy a comprehensive collection of copper pennies and halfpennies.

Chapter 18

The Investment Diamond Market – a Case of 'Caveat Emptor'

'Let the buyer beware' states the terse and unsympathetic old Latin tag, and it is difficult to find an investment market wherein sounder advice could be given. But you can certainly make money from investing in diamonds – at a diamond auction in Zurich in 1976 a Saudi Arabian jeweller paid 2,700,000 Swiss Francs for a 24.44-carat lilac-pink diamond and chalked up a new world record for a diamond price. Diamonds of quality – and that is the essential qualification – have been a good investment buy and still are, and the job of this chapter is to provide you with the basic ground rules for sensible diamond investment if you choose to allocate a chunk of your capital for this purpose. A warning note of caution at the outset, however: the diamond world, with all the glamour attached to it, is a world in which it is easy to lose a sense of proportion. In 1970 *Money Which?* bought a selection of diamonds, including loose 'investment diamonds', for £759. Twelve months later the magazine was offered £413 for the same stones. Three years later the diamonds were offered for sale again, and prices ranging from £397 to £670 were quoted for the self-same package of stones bought in 1970. In 1971 *Money Which?* bought a 1.42-carat stone for £2,595 (including £236 VAT). A week later, it tried to sell the stone back to diamond dealers. Two offers were received, one of £550, the other of £1,000.

DIAMOND PRODUCTION AND MARKETING

First, diamonds owe their value to scarcity. To start with you

125

need a temperature of 1,400° and a pressure of 600,000 atmospheres to produce a diamond. These conditions, which were provided by volcanoes venting occasional diamonds along with their lava like a tube extruding toothpaste, are extremely difficult for man to reproduce. To obtain a speck of a diamond weighing 0.2 grammes (equal to one carat, and bear in mind that 142 carats=1 ounce) man must dig out and process some 7 tons of primary deposits (those deposits nearest to their primeval source), or 20 tons of secondary deposits (diamond-bearing sediment carried away by ancient rivers).

World production of diamonds from 1970 to 1975, and the major diamond-producing areas are shown in table 11.

Table 11. *World Production of Diamonds 1974–6*

1974	1975	1976
49.84 million carats	48.16 million carats	46.86 million carats

Major diamond producers, 1976

Zaire	17	million carats
USSR	12	” ”
South Africa	7.3	” ”
Botswana	2.36	” ”
Ghana	2.22	” ”
S.W. Africa	1.69	” ”
Sierra Leone	1.09	” ”
Angola	0.4	” ”

In 1976 the total values of world sales of rough, or uncut, diamonds was $1.55 billion compared with $1.33 billion in 1973. Industrial diamonds accounted for 80 per cent of production, while 'gem' diamonds accounted for 20 per cent, but in terms of value, 'gems' accounted for 80 per cent of the market, with the biggest buyers being the US, Japan and West Germany. The demand and supply for diamonds is not quite as simple as may be supposed, because in the middle of the equation sits the De Beers' Central Selling Organisation, which was set up to establish the market back in the 1880s. Around 80 per cent of the world's rough gem and industrial diamonds are marketed through the Central Selling Organisation, which has its headquarters in London. The CSO sees its job as maintaining a steady market price for diamonds, and never to allow either a fall in the price of diamonds or an untoward price explosion. The CSO will carry stocks of diamonds at times of low demand or excess supply, and will run down the stocks when market conditions warrant. Ghana and South Africa, which do not market their output through the CSO, sell direct to dealers and merchants.

GRADING BY COLOUR

Both the European Gemmological Institute (EGI) and the Gemological Institute of America (GIA) produce gradation scales for colour (table 12). EGI use a scale which starts with 0+ for the finest stone and ranges up to 16, while GIA uses an alphabetical scale, starting with D and going up to V. In order to overcome discrepancies in gem testing between countries (such as the use of X 10 magnifying lens in the UK compared with a X 3 magnifying lens in France) the London Chamber of Commerce has a Gem Testing Laboratory which will test stones for Chamber of Commerce members. This move is all part of the international jewellers' confederation (CIBJO) which wants a common diamond-grading standard for Western Europe and South Africa.

From the colour table (table 12) you will see that only certain diamonds really qualify for investment purposes, the 'colourless' and the 'near colourless'. In buying investment diamonds, the higher up the scale your purchase is, the more likely the diamond will prove to be a good investment in terms of appreciable capital gain. 'Slightly tinted', 'very light yellow', 'light yellow' and 'yellow' stones are not suitable as investment diamonds. Even within these broad classifications there are more detailed graduations, as the table shows.

DIAMOND 'CUTS'

Next to colour comes the cut. A rough diamond is sawed, roughcut and facet-cut in five classic ways. These are: 'baguette' cut which produces a rectangular diamond; 'pear shape', which speaks for itself; 'emerald', which is an octangular cut; 'marquise', which is the shape of an elongated and

Table 12. *Classifying Diamonds by Colour*

	EGI Scale	GIA Scale	Diamonds
Colourless	0+ 0 1+	D E F	Finest white
Near Colourless	1	G	Fine white
	2	H	White
	3	I	Commercial white
	4	J	Top silver cape
Slightly Tinted	5	K	
	6	L	Silver cape
	7	M	
	8	N	Cape
Very Light Yellow	9 10 11	O P Q	Light cape
Light Yellow	12	R	
	13	S	
	14	T	
Yellow	15	U	Dark cape
	16	V	

Not suitable for investment purposes

(Source: Diamond Investors and Manufacturers AG, Diamond Centre Building, Schupstraat 9, Antwerp)

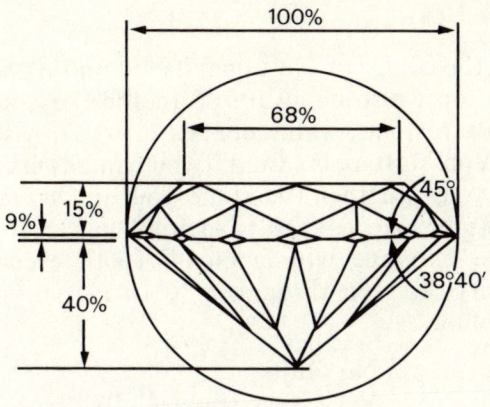

Figure 1. An ideal brilliant cut

multi-faceted rugby ball; and 'brilliant' – which is the shape that the majority of married Englishwomen prefer to have on the third finger of their left hand. Brilliant-cut diamonds are the most commonly bought investment diamond, and the cuts should be up to stringent international specification as to 'cut' proportions. An illustration of an ideal brilliant cut – in terms of proportions – is shown above (courtesy of Diamond Investors and Manufacturers).

You may wonder why the 'cut' proportions, encompassing minutiae which no layman can evaluate without specialised knowledge and equipment, are so important. The answer is that only the cuts resulting in ideal proportions for the diamond produce the maximum brilliance, or 'fire', with which to delight the eye.

Keep firmly in front of your mind that the value of a diamond is only what someone else is prepared to pay for it. Although most reputable dealers will tend to arrive at a roughly similar price for a fine white brilliant-cut stone of ideal proportions producing maximum fire or life, the buyer is entirely in the hands of the cutter, dealer or broker with whom he does business. It is not unknown for an unscrupulous dealer to overstate (sometimes by a very big margin) the value of what he is selling.

129

PURITY

Apart from the colour of the stone, its cut and its proportions, the investor must also be aware of another key factor which contributes to a stone's value or lack of it. This is the factor of 'purity'. You must assess (and if you cannot, take an expert along with you) whether the stone you are buying has any internal flaws or external faults such as 'girdle' roughness or 'colour filled cleavage with a cloud' (both evocative trade terms). Purity, as seen through a × 10 magnifying lens, is graded as follows:

F–IF .... No faults
VVS .... Very, very slight faults
VS .... Slight faults of the first degree
SI .... Slight faults of the second degree
PI .... Slight faults only just visible to the naked eye

A diamond 'fingerprint certificate' should show all its flaws unless you have been lucky enough to buy an 'F–IF' graded stone.

If you are investing in diamonds to produce a capital return, forget about made-up jewellery. The chain which leads from the diamond mine to the High Street jeweller is a long one, and each link in that chain (including wholesalers and manufacturers) will have added its particular mark-up. By the time a diamond is made up into jewellery the accumulated mark-ups may have reached up to 300 per cent. When you value your wife's diamond ring for insurance purposes do not be fooled by the valuation placed on it by a jeweller – that is for insurance premium purposes only, not a reliable guide as to what the ring may fetch if you actually have to sell it. The nearer to the diamond mine you are the less mark-up you will have to pay. Even the top diamond merchants who come to the CSO 'diamond sights' each year to haggle over wholesale diamond purchases are obliged to take parcels of assorted stones and are not allowed to pick and choose.

INVESTMENT TRENDS

Indices are, of course, produced to show how good diamonds

130

can be as an investment. One shows a price rise of over 3,000 per cent over the (curious) base year of 1940. Of course the finest white diamonds of one carat (there is little point in buying smaller stones) and over have been a good investment, and have comfortably outpaced inflation since 1970. But the key to diamond investment is grading, as even a tiny flaw can reduce the value of a stone by 20 per cent, and the biggest pitfall to watch out for is the quality of the stone itself; for this you need expert – and disinterested – advice.

Then you must remember that diamonds yield no income, only the chance of capital gain. Diamonds also have holding costs attached to them in the way of insurance and storage. Diamonds can be held in your own house, but if you are taking the precaution of insuring them, the insurance company will most likely insist on them being stored in a safe. Even then, the insurance rates will be high, particularly in fashionable areas of London. Otherwise you can keep them with your bank for a yearly charge or, a good tip this if you want to avoid paying VAT, buy the diamonds through and store them in a branch of your bank in the Channel Islands.

The last message is that diamonds are long-term investments. Do not expect to buy today and sell at a profit in six months' time. Some diamond brokers will offer to re-sell a stone after two years from the purchase date, but cannot guarantee that the price you get for it will be more than you bought it for. And do not be beguiled by the so-called 'trade prices' given by retail diamond shops in Hatton Garden. However, if we have been casting too much gloom on the diamond scene, bear in mind that the Star of South Africa, weighing 47.69 carats, was bartered in 1896 for 300 sheep, 10 oxen and a horse. In May 1974 the same stone was sold by Christie's in Geneva for £225,300 – which, you will agree, is not a bad rate of capital appreciation.

Chapter 19

Successful Investment in Silver

The British are allowed to invest in silver and, while they cannot hold gold in bar form, silver can be bought either in bar form (mainly 1,000-troy-ounce bars), as silver grain, in the form of silver coin, or as commemorative plates or medals. The speculative investment market in silver took off in a curve with a geometric rate of increase when the silver price rocketed from 90p per troy ounce in March 1973 to £3.03 per troy ounce on 26 February 1974. In the space of under twelve months an investment of £10,000 would have swollen to over £33,000 at a time when many investors were losing their shirts in the severest bear market in equities and fixed-interest stock ever experienced. The movement on the US silver market (the New York Commodity Exchange) between the high and low of the silver price on 27 and 28 February 1974 was over $1 per ounce. This movement over a two-day period was more than the *yearly* movement in the silver price range for over most of its history.

THE NATURE AND SOURCES OF SILVER

Silver is mainly a by-product of copper, zinc and lead mining. A substantial proportion of the world's silver comes from Canada, followed by Peru, Mexico, the USA and Japan. There is a substantial gap between demand for silver and the newly mined output coming on the market, and this gap is filled by recycling silver scrap, by melting down demonetised silver coin and by sales from Government stocks. Price rises or falls also entice speculative investors in silver to unload their stocks on the market and take their profits or losses. Very high price

132

levels present sufficient incentive for the vast stocks of silver held in the form of jewellery, principally in India, to be melted down and sold in bar form.

Silver is a commodity and gold is not. Therein lies the difference. Like gold, the price of silver is heavily influenced by factors such as inflation, the greed/fear ratio which is endemic to any form of speculative investment, and uncertainties about the value of paper currencies. Unlike gold, silver is not held by nations as part of their central reserves (but countries such as the USA have a strategic silver stockpile) and industrial usage of silver is much higher relative to the size of the investment market in silver than is that of gold. There is also the worry with respect to the danger of substitution – the argument being that if a huge industrial user of silver, such as Kodak or Agfa Gevaert, decided that the price of silver had reached levels rendering it uneconomic to use for production purposes, a substitute to silver would be found. There are rumours, too, that a company like Kodak must be beavering away in its research laboratories to find such a substitute.

FORCES ACTING UPON THE PRICE OF SILVER

Economic uncertainty and worry about inflation produce a natural reaction by anyone with capital to protect to hedge against depreciating paper money, equities or fixed-interest stocks. Silver is one such hedge. During 1973 and 1974 large quantities of silver passed into the hands of hoarders and, although there are a substantial number of speculative investors dealing in and out of the silver market 'on the margin', it is thought that much of silver is in strong hands, meaning that the holders have invested in silver for the long-term.

Industrial demand, the demand for silver for coinage manufacture and for silver medallions and commemorative coins all act on the price of silver, as do the silver supplies coming onto the market. Silver from mine production is increasing only slightly. Because it is a by-product, because copper, zinc and lead mines are targets of anti-pollution and conservationist lobbies, an increase in the price of silver cannot produce an immediate increase in supply. Of the other sources of supply, silver coins for melting down could be as much as 10,000 tons from the US alone, while supplies of silver are also available from the Trucial States and from India: on 22 February 1974 the Indian Government legalised exports of silver to reduce the country's balance of payments deficit and it is estimated that some 1,800 million ounces are available from this source. Poised above the silver market are the official stockpiles, the biggest of which is the US strategic stockpile estimated at 4,500 tons.

The point of constructing the scenario of the silver market in some detail and on a world-wide scale is that those who contemplate investing in silver must be aware of all factors which can affect the price. For example, if there is a heavy outflow from India or a release from the US strategic stockpile, the result would be a downward trend in the price of silver. Similarly, if Eastman Kodak discovered an economic substitute to silver, the release of the Kodak stockpile (said to be two years' supply) could also knock the silver price sharply downwards.

CHARTING THE PRICE OF SILVER

On 12 June 1968 the price of silver was at a peak of 259 old pence and by the end of 1969 the price had slumped to 156½ old pence. In 1970 and 1971 silver was in the doldrums but in 1972 and 1973 the price rose by 60 per cent in successive years against the background of currency upheavals. From a low of 82 new pence the price of silver reached £1.02 in March 1973. The price fell back to 87p per ounce during March 1973 due to the allayment of worries about the state of the foreign currency markets and rumours of a release from the US strategic stockpile. By July the price had risen to £1.17, and in August the news of the Canadian Mint's intention to mint silver coins upped the price again, while uncertainties created by the Middle East war forced silver prices on up to £1.40 by the end of December. By 26 February 1974, only two months later, the silver price had more than doubled, to £3.03 per ounce. Speculative activity, causing chaotic trading conditions, was so intense that a leading dealer commented, 'We find it impossible to predict the short-term price movement for silver, and even on an hourly basis it continues to be next to impossible.' Since the great silver boom, the price has slumped back and more orderly conditions returned to the market in 1975–8.

THE GREAT SILVER RAID

Why did it happen? The contributory cause could, if written as a novel, make a best-seller and the inevitable film might well use the appeal of Paul Newman and Robert Redford as the two stars. Fact being stranger than fiction, the 'dramatis personae' involved in The Great Silver Raid were two Texan multi-millionaires, Nelson Bunker Hunt and Herbert Hunt. Acting in unison, the brothers are believed to have entered the silver market in November 1973 and injected massive amounts of money into silver futures. By February 1974, when the ploy became more visible and other speculators jumped on the silver bandwagon, the price was moving up at the rate of 15 cents per ounce on top of each trading day's closing price to reach a peak of £3.03 (US $6.45 cents) on 26 February.

The Hunt brothers doubly disrupted the market by operating in a highly unorthodox way by taking physical delivery of the silver. Normal dealing is in silver futures, and silver futures can be bought for only 10 per cent of their value in cash, and about 95 per cent of all contracts in a normal year are liquidated before they expire. For example, a speculator or investor in silver decides to buy 10,000 ounces of silver. Instead of buying at today's price and paying cash he decides to buy on a three months forward basis, and buys at a premium of, say, just over 3 per cent. In other words, he is gambling that the price of silver will rise more during the three months than the price he is committed to pay. I say 'committed' because the speculator does not pay up for the whole amount due immediately. He pays a deposit of 20 to 25 per cent of the amount due, depending on his standing in the eye of the dealing house at the outset of the transaction. This is called dealing 'on the margin' and is familiar enough in most forms of speculative investment and particularly so in commodities. Should the price of silver fall during the three months until he is called upon to pay up the balance, he will have to 'top up' his margin.

After contracting to buy the silver, the speculator can either liquidate his position and take his profit (or loss) during or at the end of the three months, or pay up the balance of his commitment and 'take delivery'. Physically taking delivery of silver is rare because this attracts VAT. Normally silver is left in one of the terminal markets, ie. with one of the members of the London Silver Market or with one of the traders on the London Metal Exchange.

The Hunt brothers' doubly disrupting the market wrought havoc among silver speculators at the time who had, as was their wont, sold short to take advantage of the previous discount of the cash price against the forward quotation. However, the Hunts' manoeuvres at one stage forced the spot price of silver in New York to a premium over the forward price as a result of a scarcity of readily accessible supplies.

By the 'Great Silver Raid', the Hunt brothers could have made $150 million (on paper at least) at the peak of the silver price boom. If they bought on the margin and used their silver as 'geared up' collateral for borrowing, the Hunts may have been, and maybe still are, genuinely convinced of the merits of silver as a long-term medium of investment with which to hedge part of their massive fortunes against inflation. However, their presence in the market creates great uncertainty as no-one is sure whether the Hunts intend to remain long-term holders of the metal, or were simply driving the price up to hold industry to ransom. The price was indeed driven up to such an extent that the silver market ceased to obey rational principles and the price became wildly out of touch with fundamentals.

Since the 'Great Silver Raid' there has been a return to more normal conditions in the silver market and, assuming that the Hunts are still holding their stocks, the overall profitability of the exercise is open to question.

THE MECHANICS OF THE MARKET PLACE

The traditional London Silver Market is made up of three members – Sharps, Pixley; Mocatta & Goldsmid; and Samuel Montagu. Representatives of the three bullion houses meet at 12 noon each working day to hold the price 'fixing' at which the demand for and supply of silver by their respective clients is balanced. The London Silver Market can supply clients almost anywhere in the world with orders of over 1,000 ounces. It can deal in any currency, in forward positions of up to a year, and charges brokerage of ¼ per cent on purchases only.

The London Metal Exchange started dealing in silver in 1968 for the first time since 1939, this being the LME's third attempt to establish trading in silver since the war. Four trading sessions in silver are held each day, and ¼ per cent brokerage on both sales and purchases is charged by the traders. The first London Metal Exchange silver market started in 1897 and closed in 1911 because of lack of interest. The second market opened in 1935 but failed to re-open after the war. The LME was finally released from controls in 1953, mainly because of the post-war policy of the US Treasury in virtually freezing the price of silver by guaranteeing to supply buyers at the fixed price of $1.29 a troy ounce – a policy abandoned by the US on 18 May 1968 due to pressure from speculators and consumers. It was generally recognised at that time that silver was no longer a monetary metal since most countries had abandoned using silver coinage and thus silver lent itself to being traded freely on the LME alongside base metals. However, the re-entry of the LME as a second market in silver in London stimulated the traditional bullion dealers to widen dealings in their own markets, and the daily fixing was changed to cover not only spot and three months but also six months and one year.

Silver has not quite the glamour of gold, indeed a stack of silver 10,000-ounce bars is reminiscent of a pile of breeze blocks, while gold certainly looks like gold with its rich yellow sheen. However, silver is still a long way from being a 'base' metal. It is important to remember that UK residents investing in silver must deal in sizeable amounts, starting at a minimum of 5,000 ounces. At over £2 an ounce, a few pence change in the price either way can produce hefty profits or losses.

Chapter 20

Stamps as an Inflation Beater

Those tiny pieces of paper, usually perforated, known as postage stamps form one of the less traditional sectors of the investment world. But just to whet your appetite, the British Guiana One Cent Black on Magenta of 1856, which is the world's most valuable stamp and probably the most valuable single item in the world in terms of size and weight, is now worth some £300,000, £75,000 more than its value a year ago. The One Cent, which is unique, is currently owned by an American investment syndicate who paid £116,666 for it at an auction in New York's Waldorf-Astoria Hotel on 24 March 1970. One other appetite sharpener: when asked by the *Sunday Times* what his best investment had proved to be, Maxwell Joseph, the Chairman of the Grand Metropolitan Hotels Group, replied unhesitatingly, 'My stamp collection.'

The facts bear him out. In 1973 Stanley Gibbons selected thirteen classic stamps and now values them each year. The 1972–3 value of the thirteen stamps was £82,940, by the following year it had jumped to £106,950, in 1974–5 the value of the thirteen stamps had reached £130,855, by 1975–6, £163,175 and by 1976–7 £202,680. In a period during which the value of ordinary shares collapsed – the *Financial Times* 30-share index reached 146.6 at the beginning of January 1975 – and virtually every other investment sector, including the tried and true investment in bricks, mortar and land, witnessed drastic downward movement, stamps went on steadily rising in value. They have risen in value not only in nominal terms, but also in real terms. As can be seen from the figures above, the latest increase in the value of the 'thirteen-stamp portfolio'

138

was 24 per cent over 1975–6 and 25 per cent for the preceding year, so the stamps have provided a real increase over and above the rapid rate of inflation.

THE STRENGTHS OF THE STAMP MARKET

Why? There appears to be three basic reasons for the strength of the stamp market. One reason is provided by the fact that the stamp market is not subject to the volatility of other investment markets because investors make up only a small proportion of the market. Most people who buy stamps are collectors, who are not going to be lured into unloading a Twopenny Blue, or their 1847 Trinidad Five Cents Blue, just because they have gone up in value. For one thing they are bitten by the collecting bug, so they get a good dollop of psychological income from poring over their treasures; for another, what is the sense in exchanging a tiny but appreciating piece of paper for a sizeable chunk of fast depreciating (and not so picturesque) sterling? Even investors can get bitten by the collecting bug: most investors who put aside a slice of their capital to invest in a portfolio of stamps, if they do then sell their stamps in response to a tempting offer, usually re-invest the proceeds in more stamps. So the stamp market is firmly underpinned against the type of sudden exodus – remember Chinese ceramics or even Scotch whisky? – which leaves the less fleet of foot holding the unwanted baby.

Another reason why stamps have outpaced the market place is because the market for stamps is international: you will get the same price for your stamps in London or Paris or New York or Hong Kong. This presents the investor with an excellent inflation hedge, particularly against a downward spiral of sterling like that which took place during 1974 to early 1977. Stamps can be converted into dollars or Swiss francs or German marks and, if you intend to quit these shores one day, your stamp collection forms part and parcel of your personal possessions along with your car, furniture, etc. This means you can take it along with you at the time you actually leave the UK instead of leaving it behind with the bulk of your sterling assets for the four years' restriction period laid down by the Exchange Control Act 1947.

This brings us on to the next point. Stamps are very small, and as such are easily transportable, which makes them attractive as an investment for those who want to cross frontiers and take their wealth along with them. The Director of one of the UK's biggest bullion dealers, asked what the effect of the quadrupled Arab oil revenues would be on the price of gold if the Arabs decided to invest in the yellow metal, replied tersely, 'They won't.' For the Arabs to translate some of that cash into gold seemed to be a logical thing to do at the time, but the reason why they did not was that they did not like the thought of lugging large chunks of gold around if they were forced to leave their country in a hurry. Nor did they like the thought of lodging it in a bank vault in another country, just in case they ran the risk of expropriation.

MEASURING PERFORMANCE

Table 13 lists the thirteen classic stamps in the Gibbons investment portfolio: they are rather akin, in the stamp world, to the *Financial Times* 30-share index in that they provide a device to monitor the state of the stamp market.

The prices of classic stamps are mainly affected by supply and demand as one would expect. Supply cannot increase and demand has been on the increase, fuelled both by the collectors and the investors across the world. But, as in all markets, some sections of the market rise faster than others. Stanley Gibbons recommend for investment purposes classic stamps and other stamps issued up to 1900, although the firm will sometimes also suggest carefully selected stamps issued up to 1930. There is a heavy demand for British stamps of all periods, but particularly for those issued during the reigns of Queen Victoria, Edward VII and George V. In the Great Britain section of Gibbons' latest British Commonwealth Catalogue, unused stamps of Queen Victoria's reign have risen by approximately 69 per cent since the previous year's edition, while stamps issued during the reign of Edward VII have increased by 60 per cent and stamps of George V's era by 72 per cent. Some of the rises of fairly classic stamps are shown below:

Table 13. The Stanley Gibbons Investment Portfolio

STAMPS	1962	1968	1972	1973	1974–5	1975–6	1976–7
German States (Saxony) 1850 3 pf. corner block of six	–	£28,000	£35,000*	£50,000*	£62,500*	£75,000	£80,000
Mauritius 1847 2d Post Office	£5,000	£13,000	£22,500	£27,000	£33,000	£45,000	£67,500
Austrian 1851 (6 Kr)	£2,500	£4,500	£6,000	£7,000	£8,500	£10,500	£14,500
Great Britain 1910 King Edward VII 2d 'Tyrian Plum'	£1,250	£1,750	£3,000	£3,500	£4,000	£4,500	£5,500
Great Britain 1867–83 Queen Victoria £5	£375	£700	£1,750	£2,000	£2,500	£3,000	£4,500
Cape of Good Hope 1861 1d 'Woodblock'	£500	£700	£1,800	£2,000	£2,500	£3,750	£5,000
New Hebrides 1908 1d error overprint omitted on Fiji in pair with normal	£175	£450	£1,300	£1,500	£1,750	£2,000	£2,600
Norway 1855 4 Sk	£95	£400	£700	£900	£1,100	£1,250	£1,500
France 1869 5 Fr Napoleon	£100	–	£400	£475	£650	£850	£1,100
South Africa 1913 £1 King George V	£24	£50	–	£100	£130	£300	£350
Great Britain 1d Black	£28	£38	£90	£125	£175	£275	£430
Australia 1913 £2 'Kangaroo'	£50	£175	£300	£350	£550	£750	£1,200
Great Britain 1904 6d IR Official	–	£3,800	£10,000	£12,000	£13,500	£16,000	£18,500

* estimated

(figures by courtesy of Stanley Gibbons International Ltd)

141

		1975	*1976*
2d Blue 1840	unused	£450	£600
	used	£35	£60
1d Red from Plate 77	unused	£5,000	£8,000
	used	£3,500	£6,000
£1 Brown Lilac of 1884	unused	£500	£750

It will be seen that there is a vast difference in the value of stamps depending on whether they are 'used' or 'unused'. Equally, collectors pore over stamps to ascertain which particular plate was used in the printing process. A Penny Black from one plate can be worth much more than a Penny Black printed on another. So the investor without specialist knowledge would be well advised to obtain expert opinions before paying over hard cash.

Commonwealth stamps are also in vogue, as some examples below show:

		1975	*1976*
British Guiana 2 Cents Rose 1851	used	£15,000	£20,000
Falkland Island 1861–77 Red frank on cover	used	£2,500	£3,500
Canada 1851 12d Black	unused	£14,000	£18,000
Bermuda 1854 1d 'Perot' Red/Blue	used	£50,000	£60,000

Other Commonwealth pre-1900 issues have shown the same trend, and there is also considerable continuing demand for stamps of the USA and of European countries.

STAMP INVESTMENT MANAGERS

Four years ago Stanley Gibbons (Drury House, Russell Street, London WC2; 01-836 8444) set up an investment service for those who were interested more in seeing their stamps increase in value than in the sheer joy of collecting stamps. The minimum investment in a stamp portfolio is £500, and when Stanley Gibbons place stamp investments in the medium to long-term category, this means that you are expected to hold your investment for five to ten years. The 'front-end loading'

(Stanley Gibbons' profit margin) is charged at the outset of the relationship, so this cost has to be spread over a number of years. Normally the mark-up is around 10 per cent. Where an investment is over £5,000, Stanley Gibbons will store your collection, for a small fee, in one of their vaults, and this includes also the cost of insuring them. No charge is paid for advice on investment. Other stamp investment services include those run by Warwick & Warwick (Philately) Ltd (Graphic House, 35–7 Albert Street, Rugby, Warwicks; 0788 65430) and by Urch Holdings Ltd (9 Christmas Steps, Bristol; 0272 20442).

Chapter 21

Successful Investment in Hand-Made Carpets

A good off-beat investment opportunity lies in hand-made carpets from the Middle and Far East. Most 'investment' carpets on the market date from 1880 to 1930, and are still in the same price range as newly made hand-woven carpets. The difference is that, although standards of workmanship in new carpets are high, new carpets do not have the same strength and durability because the weavers are not using the same wools. Modern hand-made carpets are increasingly woven from imported wools of softer texture than the wools of the old carpets, which came from the country of origin. Again, modern wools are dyed with modern chemicals which lack the subtlety of traditional vegetable dyes.

The best carpets still have not reached the prices paid for them in the 1920s, inflation notwithstanding, but prices at the top end of the carpet market are high. For example, £58,000 was realised in a recent Islamic sale for a seventeenth century silk and wool reversible rug. This is the sort of rug which is made from hand-knotting wool or silk around foundation threads with some 600 knots per square inch, giving it a life of a century or more even when in use on the floor – though a sensible investor paying out that sort of money would either keep his carpet in bond (as do the Swiss, to avoid paying any import duty) if he is prepared to forgo the aesthetic pleasure it can give him, or hang it on a wall.

Other advantages of carpets as an investment are that they do not break, burglars do not normally recognise their value, and obviously they are difficult to lose (unlike stamps or coins).

DEALER, AUCTION OR BROKER

There are three ways of setting about carpet investment. First, you can buy from a dealer, but you could pay 50 per cent or more of the carpet's value to the dealer on his mark-up, so you would have to wait for quite some time before your investment began to show a realisable profit. Next, you can buy at the major auction houses of Sotheby's, Christie's or Phillips. Here again, a buyer's premium (10 per cent) and a seller's premium (10 per cent) are charged at auction, which inflates the price by 20 per cent. So again you would have to wait quite a while before your purchase covered its cost through capital appreciation.

The third and possibly the best alternative is to use a broker who has access to the bonded carpet warehouses which have recently moved from the five and a half acres in Bishopsgate in the City leased to them by the Port of London Authority to three different premises: one in North London (the International Oriental Carpet Centre) and two in the City of London. A broker such as Caroline Bosly (13 Princess Road, Regent's Park, London NW1) has access to these bonded carpet warehouses, access which the average member of the public does not have. These bonded carpet warehouses should not be confused with advertised 'special rug auctions'. A few of the latter are indeed run by old-established firms but there is an analogy with Hatton Garden 'trade prices' for diamonds and other precious stones. In most cases the investor thinking he is getting something cheap ends up paying more than the retail price for the same carpet or rug.

After all, with carpet prices rising steadily, no auctioneer will sell good rugs at silly prices. And if you go to an auction at which no dealers are present, you can fairly safely bet that prices are so high that it is not worth a dealer's while to attend: he is content to leave the bidding to gullible members of the public.

LONDON IS THE HUB

Most of the world's carpet trade passes through London, through the bonded warehouses which exist for dealers only, except in cases where brokers buy on your behalf for a commission, and indeed 97 per cent of the carpets passing through are re-exported without ever leaving bond.

London's pre-eminence·as a hand-made carpet centre dates back some fifty years when a wholesale Persian and Oriental carpet market was established by a number of Armenian, Persian, Turkish and Russian families who took up residence in Britain. The Port of London Authority leased huge warehouses to them and these were stocked with many millions of pounds worth of fine hand-made rugs and carpets of every size, colour and variety.

When rugs and carpets arrive in London from the main producing countries, which include Iran, Turkey, Afghanistan, Russia, India, Pakistan, China, Romania and Egypt, they are inspected, sorted, graded and washed prior to being re-exported (except for the 3 per cent that remain in Britain). Because the warehouses are in bond – a kind of free-trade zone – rugs for re-export are not liable for any UK duty or VAT unless bought by a UK resident or by a dealer for on-sale to a UK resident.

The reason for the existence of the carpet centre in London is simple. It fulfils the prime function of a market because it brings together rugs and carpets from many different rug-weaving areas. Few dealers could afford to travel every few months to Iran, Turkey, Pakistan, Afghanistan or China. Instead they just make the one trip every few months to the London bonded warehouses. Here the trade prices are normally lower than those charged in the areas where the rugs and carpets are made. The reason for this seeming anomaly is that a rug or carpet takes months or even years to weave. The craftsmen and workshops cannot finance themselves for these long periods, so the London importers subsidise them by paying for their carpets in advance at prices considerably lower than those at which the rugs are on offer in the local trading bazaar.

For the investor, the only route into the bonded warehouses is through a broker who deals in large quantities of carpets and rugs with wholesalers in this country and abroad. But the broker will also come to an arrangement with the principal importing firms to enable him to sell to private individuals as well. Anybody who is after a specific size, colour, pattern or price bracket can go to a broker who will obtain the carpet

– for a small percentage on each deal – from a bonded warehouse. Most brokers are as willing to procure cheapish, colourful rugs starting at perhaps £50 as they are to search out investment rugs costing many thousands of pounds. A broker will advise you on whether a rug is a good example of its type and whether it should wear well. As rugs are priced according to the bale (ie. everything in one bale will be the same price per square foot) it is important to know whether you are getting the best or the worst of the bale.

Some idea of the price difference between buying through a broker and from a store is given by this example. A silk rug from Iran could be bought through a broker for about £900 plus VAT. The same rug will be selling in UK stores for around £2,000 while in France, Belgium and Germany (where the higher duty applies) the same rug will cost nearer £3,000.

INVESTMENT TIPS

The best advice an investor can have is to buy the best rug at the best price. This may seem obvious but there can be a 20 per cent difference in the prices asked for nearly identical rugs or carpets by different importers within the same bonded warehouse. You will not know it at the time but you will when you eventually come to sell the rug or carpet.

If you fancy a small investment, you can buy a perfectly good Beluchi rug measuring 5ft by 3ft for a little over £100. Beluchis are made in Afghanistan or Iran by the nomadic tribes which wander back and forth over the frontier. Do not worry too much about the symmetry of the shape; just ensure that it is soundly made.

In the medium-price range, it is worth looking at Turkish Kula wool rugs – one exception to the rule that the best investment is in old rugs only. These are woven in soft colours, are hard-wearing and are well made, with runners narrow enough to fit narrow halls. A coffee-table rug would cost around £226, while room-sized carpets cost around £1,000.

For those with more to invest, a Silk Qum is recommended. For a 4ft 6in. by 2ft 6in. rug you would pay around £900; for a 5ft 6in. by 3ft 9in. rug you would pay around £1,500 to £1,600. You can keep such a rug on the floor of a room which is not too much trodden upon (definitely not a playroom) or preferably put it on the wall. To hang such a rug on the wall, sew on wide webbing along the top and bottom of the rug, using big tacking stitches, and then slip a brass rod through the open ends of the webbing. Another good buy is an Isfahan rug, about the same price as Qum.

For the really big investor a Silk Hereke, which has 600 knots per square inch (the finest rug ever discovered had 1,200 knots) is recommended. Cost: from £6,000 to £10,000.

If you want to make sure that any rug is genuinely hand-made look at the back of the rug. If you can see the design, then the rug is most probably hand-made. If you cannot, then it is definitely not hand-made.

THE THREE SECTORS

The hand-made carpet market falls into three parts:

1. Turkish and Caucasian, Afghan, Turkestan and East Turkestan carpets have bold, almost coarse, geometrical patterns that blend well with the modern furniture. In this sector only the classical sixteenth and seventeenth century Turkish and Caucasian carpets are of interest to the investor. There is a small cult buying interest in Tribal rugs by young, rich Americans who may have made (or want to be thought to have made) a trip down the hippie trail to Afghanistan.

2. A much better sector for the prudent investor is the Persian hand-made carpet – with its fine weave and delicate scrollwork patterns of fragile blossoms and tendrils. These carpets look well with period furniture, whether Georgian, Regency or French. Some specialists say that these carpets are bound to leap in price because the weavers in Iran are deserting their looms and pushing off to get the higher pay offered by the oil fields. Hence, scarcity lies ahead. But another school of thought reckons that the Shah of Iran wants to keep a viable Persian carpet industry in being against the time when the oil wells run dry. So the Shah has pushed up the weavers' wages to make sure that not too many of them leave their looms.

A bull point in favour of hand-made Persian carpets is that the oil revenues of Iran and other Middle Eastern oil states have put vast amounts of cash into the hands of individuals who wish to buy back their own cultural heritage, part of which consists of the old rugs and carpets of the country concerned. So far, the oil sheiks have been buying carpets of 1920s vintage, which means that there still is not much of a premium between the older Persian carpets and rugs and those of the 1920s. Once the loophole is spotted and exploited, the premium for the old carpets should rise substantially.

Currently the price of modern Persian carpets on the British market is £600 per square metre. Due to inflation, plus the higher wage-scale introduced by the Shah, manufacturers are seeking £1,000 per square metre for new carpets and are projecting a price level of £2,000 per square metre in the near future, so the astute investor buying now should reap a substantial reward in a relatively short period.

3. The third sector of the carpet market is made by the Chinese and other Far Eastern carpets and old European carpets. Here, prices are boosted by rarity value and because wealthy individuals like to furnish period homes with furniture and carpets of the same period.

THE TEST OF TIME

Do investment carpet prices stand the test of time? Table 14 is made up of figures supplied by Jack Franses of Sotheby's, showing selected hand-made carpet price movements between 1951 and 1975.

CHEAPER RELATION?

Some final advice for the amateur investor in carpets:

1. If the type of carpet you want is too much for your pocket, then investigate its regional group more closely to see if it has a more modestly priced near-relation. For example, if you like the colour and design of an (expensive) Tabriz, you might well find a cheaper Kurdish of similar design and appeal.

2. When you are buying look at the condition of the carpet. Beware of repairs and weak areas. These are expensive to put right. Do not be put off by dirt: cleaning is inexpensive, but let the experts do it. Do not try it yourself.

149

Table 14. Prices of Selected Hand-Made Carpets 1951–75

Rug	Size	Circa	1951 £	1961 £	1971 £	1973 £	1974 £	1975 £
Beluchistan	5ft 8in.×3ft 6in.	1900	20	50	130	165	265	265
Beluchistan	5ft×3ft 6in.	1870	25	35	180	295	495	495
Chichi	6ft×4ft 3in.	1800	45	120	900	1,500	2,500	2,500
Dagestan	9ft×4ft 10in.	1840	40	110	450	950	1,500	2,000
Dagestan prayer	5ft×4ft	1860	30	60	250	600	1,200	2,000
Shirvan (Konagkend)	6ft 2in.×4ft 5in.	1860	55	145	750	1,300	2,200	3,000
Joshagan	7ft×4ft	1830	150	350	1,200	2,500	2,800	3,500
Kirman	7ft 8in.×4ft 5in.	1850	120	250	750	1,250	1,800	2,500
Ispahan	7ft 6in.×4ft 7in.	1890	200	450	1,200	2,200	2,900	3,500
Raised silk Kashan	6ft 8in.×4ft 6in.	1870	100	275	1,200	2,500+	4,500	4,500
Sehna Kelim	6ft 6in.×4ft 6in.	1820	20	60	250	450	450	600
Shiraz	6ft 6in.×4ft 4in.	1830	80	140	800	1,500	2,200	2,200
Pende prayer	6ft×4ft 5in.	1820	50	130	650	1,200	3,000	3,000
Makri prayer	7ft×4ft 3in.	1800	100	350	950	1,500+	3,000	5,000
Melas prayer	5ft 4in.×3ft 9in.	1800	125	250	950	2,000	3,500	5,000
Kula	6ft 8in.×4ft 2in.	1760	150	250	1,250	1,800	1,800	2,800
Kazak	8ft 2in.×3ft 10in.	1840	60	250	950	1,800	2,800	3,500

3. Once you have obtained the rug of your choice, then keep it clean by using a damp soapy sponge for stains and a brush or vacuum cleaner to get rid of dust. Do not use bleach or harsh cleaners. Better still, send your rug for the occasional clean-up by a specialist Oriental carpet cleaner.

Chapter 22

Successful Investment in Agricultural Land

As with any investment sector, general movements of agricultural land prices over a long period of time can conceal considerable variations within short time-spans and within particular sectors of the market. This chapter therefore divides the UK market in agricultural land into 'vacant possession' land, 'tenanted' land, 'land and buildings' and 'land only', and traces the movement of land prices within these segments since 1971. It also examines land price variations between different areas of the country. The figures are given in acres, but latterly the Ministry of Agriculture has been providing land statistics in hectares rather than acres. This is not only due to the metrication programme, but also because the use of hectares facilitates comparison with EEC statistics. But acres enable you to assess the price trend lines over a period of time in a common unit of measurement, and are still a great deal easier to visualise and to understand than are hectares. In fact, 1 hectare equals 2.4711 acres.

THE AGRICULTURAL LAND MARKET 1971–8

The agricultural land market reached a peak in the period October 1973 to March 1974, when the price of land reached an average of £612 an acre, an increase of 260 per cent over the period from 1965–6 when the price of land was £170. Agricultural land prices then fell away during the financial traumas and property crises of 1975 and 1976. and bottomed out at £435 an acre in the period October 1975 to March 1976. Since then, as more normal conditions returned to the

152

market, the price of agricultural land started to climb again, particularly during the latter half of 1977 and the first half of 1978, to reach an average price of £985 an acre by the beginning of 1978. Over the whole period from 1965 to 1978 the price of land has risen by 479 per cent, from £170 per acre to £985. However, average land prices are a pretty rough and ready method of evaluating market trends. The size of the unit of land sold, whether the land is sold on a tenanted basis or with vacant possession, whether the land has buildings on it, the quality of the land, climate, the existence of fixed equipment – all these factors have a bearing on the price at which land is bought and sold.

'VACANT POSSESSION' LAND SALES

Table 15 provides the figures for agricultural land, from units of 10 acres and upwards, for the half-year ended 1971 compared with the six months ended 30 September 1977.

As you can see, it is the smaller agricultural units (up to 49 acres) which cost highest per acre. The price of £979 per acre in sector 1 is also high when we compare it with the price of £570 per acre for small units of tenanted land and buildings, shown in table 16 below. As a general rule, as we move up the price scale price per acre drops and the influence of the farm building value on the value of the overall unit being sold naturally diminishes, so if you are buying farm buildings together with land, the lesson of the last seven years is that you tend to get a better deal the larger the unit you are able to invest in. However, pride of place for capital appreciation is taken by farms in the 50–99 acre category, which showed a 234 per cent increase over the period, as against a growth rate of 161 per cent for the large size (300 acres plus) farms.

When we come to 'land only' sales, in sector 2, offered for sale with vacant possession, the same pattern repeats itself, with the 1977 price per acre falling away from £658 for the small acreage unit to £122 for units in excess of 300 acres. As you can readily see from comparing the 'land only' prices with those for 'land and buildings', the premium per acre paid for the buildings is at its highest for the smaller size units as one would naturally expect. In terms of capital appreciation, the

Table 15. *Land Sold with Vacant Possession*

Size group acres	Average price per acre 1971	Average price per acre 1977	% increase
Sector 1			
Land and buildings	£	£	
10–49	303	979	223%
50–99	204	681	234%
100–149	174	570	228%
150–299	202	552	173%
300 and over	184	481	161%
all areas	205	599	192%
Sector 2			
Land only			
10–49	208	658	216%
50–99	199	585	194%
100–149	217	518	139%
150–299	139	541	289%
300 and over	99	122	23%
all areas	187	550	194%
Sector 3			
All properties			
10–49	284	749	202%
50–99	202	640	217%
100–149	185	558	202%
150–299	192	550	186%
300 and over	175	415	137%
all areas	199	582	192%

(Source: *Sales of Agricultural Land in England and Wales*, published by the Ministry of Agriculture)

most spectacular capital gains are recorded by the smaller units, reflecting not only the increase in the value of the land but also the effect of the upsurge in property prices over the period.

The same pattern is repeated in sector 3, which encompasses 'all properties', with the price per acre dropping steadily away as the acreage of the unit increases, with or without buildings. Again, the largest capital gain is chalked up by agricultural units in the 10–100 acre category.

TENANTED LAND

There is a big difference between the price of land with vacant

Table 16. *Tenanted Land Sales*

Size group acres	Average price per acre 1971	Average price per acre 1977	% increase
Sector 1			
Land and buildings	£	£	
10–49	173	570	229%
50–99	123	374	204%
100–149	100	362	262%
150–299	133	379	185%
300 and over	173	405	134%
all areas	143	397	178%
Sector 2			
Land only			
10–49	151	478	217%
50–99	164	469	186%
100–149	190	n.a.	—
150–299	184	n.a.	—
300 and over	n.a.	n.a.	—
all areas	165	340	106%
Sector 3			
All properties			
10–49	160	522	226%
50–99	135	395	193%
100–149	106	374	253%
150–299	140	357	155%
300 and over	173	399	131%
all areas	146	393	169%

possession and tenanted land prices, and over the years the differential has been maintained. The capital gain made by tenanted land, together with buildings, of the small variety (10–49 acres) shows much the same capital appreciation as the same size units sold with vacant possession.

LESSONS TO BE LEARNED

What are the lessons to be learned from this welter of statistics? The first is that it is difficult to lose money on agricultural land over the longer term. However, you can lose money if you buy at the wrong time and are forced to sell in the short term. Those who bought in the winter of 1973, when agricultural land prices stood at an average of £612 per acre, were nursing their losses when they sold in 1976 when the average price had dropped to £460 per acre. Had they hung on until 1978, when the price reached £985 per acre, they would have made a reasonable capital gain from their investment. Still, even in the bleak years of 1975 and 1976 you could have taken comfort from the fact that you would not have lost as much money on agricultural land as you would have lost having invested in a representative selection of blue-chip shares over the same period.

Over the long term, land is a good investment. It produces not only income but also capital gain, and as one old Taunton Vale farmer said to me in a dialect I cannot reproduce, 'Land can't run away'. The land market occasionally produces sudden bursts of excitement when land prices surge strongly ahead over quite short periods, as was the case in the latter half of 1977 and the beginning of 1978. Measured over a sustained period of years, and taking the good years with the bad, you would have to be very unfortunate in your timing to lose money by investment in agricultural land.

REGIONAL VARIATIONS

There are, of course, considerable regional variations in agricultural land prices reflecting quality of land and the other salient factors. These are shown in table 17 for selected areas of the UK, based on all sales of land and buildings both with vacant possession and on a tenanted basis.

The most expensive land is in the West Midlands. Contrast the price levels in the latter area with, say, land prices in Wales or the North.

However, if you are thinking of opting out for the rural life, bear in mind that life can be hard on a small Welsh hill farm – and while the views can be panoramic the capital appreciation can be low compared with that of the fertile lowland. The other point to remember is that you should try if possible to purchase the bigger units of farmland – 50 acres plus – because you can pay nearly double the price per acre for the small farms. Agriculture is one industry wherein, for the buyer at least, there are economies of scale.

Table 17. *Sales of Agricultural Land by Selected Areas*

(Average price per acre at 30 September '77)

Size group acres	South West	Wales	South Eastern	Eastern	West Midland	North	Yorks/ Lancs
10–49	720	634	805	698	858	666	667
50–99	588	398	684	690	787	521	570
100–149	571	344	585	603	599	398	585
150–299	549	290	537	554	607	302	483
300 & over	590	139	463	486	455	267	195
all sizes	611	392	591	563	656	390	412

WHAT ABOUT TAX?

When it comes to capital transfer tax, the working farmer – that is the chap who actually works the land in which he has invested capital as opposed to the absentee landlord – is fairly liberally treated. When transferring his land as a gift to his heirs he qualifies for 'special agricultural relief' and gets a discount of 50 per cent of the market value of his farm for CTT purposes. There is a cut-off point for this relief, which currently stands at 1,000 acres or £250,000 in value. This means that the working farmer attracts the 50 per cent discount on CTT up to this acreage or value but not beyond. However, the working farmer with an agricultural unit in excess of the cut-off points can also claim a 'business relief' of a 30 per cent discount on the market value of the acreage in excess of 1,000 acres or over the £250,000 value figure.

The working farmer also gains relief from CGT liability, and that runs at 50 per cent. For most farmers CGT on the remaining half is not a formidable deterrent either, as they are entitled to 'retirement relief' of £20,000 plus the offsets of 'property enhancement' reliefs. No gains tax whatsoever is charged on a farm unit if the farmer dies in possession, but there is a somewhat heavier CTT liability in this event.

Even with the reliefs however, there has been a swing among farm owners to running the enterprise under the shelter of a trust or within a corporate structure which can, in theory, never die. This puts such farmers on a more competitive footing as against the institutional investors such as pension funds.

157

For the land owner who is not a working farmer there is no special relief against either capital transfer tax or capital gains tax. However, this penalty is reflected in the considerable price differential, already noted, between 'vacant possession' land and tenanted land.

Bear in mind, too, that land is a major investment and it does not pay to be too greedy. Remember what happened to Jim 'Stop-at-the-sea' Slater who got badly stuck long before his farmland buying reached the Channel. Land is essentially a long-term investment for prudent and well-heeled investors.

Chapter 23

Successful Investment in Woodlands

Investment in woodlands is not fully understood by many, both individuals and companies, who could best benefit from it. For those with earned and unearned incomes wilting under a penal rate of tax, and having capital to pass on to the next generation, investment in forestry means that you can create woodlands at the expense of the Inland Revenue and increase your after tax income at the same time. You can also roll up your eventual capital transfer tax liability into the distant future and, equally important, substantially ameliorate its effects. In addition you can obtain the psychological income from feeling that you have improved the landscape – as long as you do not follow the Forestry Commission's policy of planting those gloomy landscapes of drab conifers slashed vertically and horizontally by regimented firebreaks. Lastly, there is a 'perk' from investing in woodlands in that you can have a house built on the woodland area for holiday use. This is allowable as an expense against tax in that you can show that it is part and parcel of your timber management business.

SUPPLY AND DEMAND

Investment in woodland is fundamentally no different from other forms of investment in that the price of woodland is governed by supply and demand, and it is on the increase in price per acre that your capital gain depends. For the statistics on the woodland 'market', we are indebted to the Investment and Economics Department of Economic Forestry Limited (Hillgate House, 26 Old Bailey, London EC4M 7LT and at 27 Rutland Square, Edinburgh 1).

159

Successful Investment

For a crowded island, Britain has a remarkable number of trees but has the capacity for a great deal more. The economic case for improving Britain's self-sufficiency in timber is clear enough. The Department of Trade statistics show that after machinery, fuel and food, timber is Britain's fourth biggest import bill. Our daily consumption of imported timber is at the rate of £4 million a day, and our timber imports have shot up in recent years. It is clearly in the interests of our balance of payments to replace imported timber with the home-produced variety but, as with many other areas, the British have reacted late in the day to changing circumstances. Until comparatively recently, the business of woodland creation was left to the resident landowner. The First World War so depleted Britain's reserves of timber that the Forestry Commission was set up in 1919. It has now created 2 million acres of stocked woodland. However, despite the work of the Forestry Commission and of private growers, only 3½ million acres of Britain's woodlands are productive out of total woodland stocks of nearly 5 million acres due to our late start in re-afforestation. With new woodlands being planted at the rate of 94,000 acres each year, the British woodland area still represents only 8 per cent of the land surface – principally in Scotland, the north and north-west of England, Wales and the West Country – as against the West European average of 22 per cent. One obvious area for expansion is the marginal hill lands, much of which were brought into agricultural use during the last war and continue to be farmed with the aid of subsidies and grants. This land – nearly 14 million acres – produces low agricultural yields, principally from sheep farming, and a reasonable proportion of the area could be given over to forestry land.

WOODLANDS AS AN INVESTMENT

Woodlands viewed purely as an investment have stood the test of time well. Table 18 shows over a fifty-year span (timber is essentially a long-term investment) the mean values per acre for the most widely planted coniferous woodlands at 1976 price levels. The table is not intended to show the market value of any one plantation but provides a general guide to values.

Focusing now on the income produced from woodland (upon

Table 18. *Woodland Values over a Fifty-year Life Span*

	10 years	15 years	20 years	25 years	30 years	35 years
£ per acre	100	200	290	410	550	640

	40 years	45 years	50 years
£ per acre	890	1,100	1,500

which the capital values depend), the graph below shows the price movement of home-grown softwood, of imported softwood, and hill land between 1963 and 1975 compared, on an index basis (with 1963=100) with the *Financial Times* all share index. The imported softwood index is supplied by the

FIGURE 2

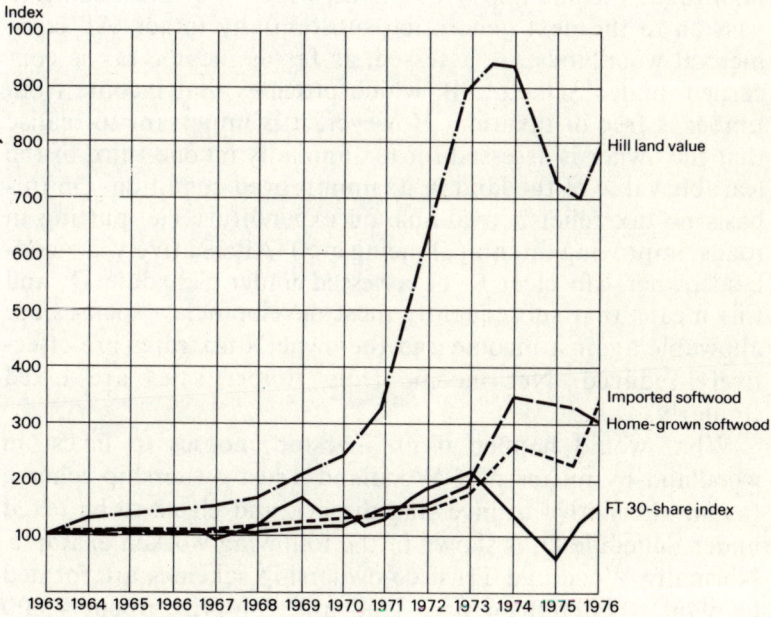

Comparative performances of timber, hill land
and the Stock Exchange 1963–74

161

Timber Trade Federation, the home-grown softwood index is supplied by the Forestry Commission and the hill land value index is an average of the Forestry Commission records, the Economic Forestry Group records and the Country Landowners Association statistics.

It is essential to understand (and this cannot be over-emphasised) that forestry is a long-term investment which provides a steady return averaging 5 per cent compound on the rotation of the timber felled and sold. This return should be protected against inflation in future by the cost of imported lumber and pulp – increasing costs which are the main inflationary influences on home timber prices.

TAX BENEFITS

Another determinant of forestry land prices is provided by the tax benefits which are of particular attraction to those with high taxed income and with capital which they are hoping to pass on to the next generation substantially intact. All commercial woodlands are assessed, as far as income tax is concerned, under Schedule B, which provides that income from timber is free of taxation. However, it is important to realise that the owner is assessed for tax annually on one-third of the leasable value of the land in its unimproved condition. On this basis no tax relief is available on expenditure (ie. putting in roads, improving ditching, fencing etc.). Alternatively, a woodland owner can elect to be assessed under Schedule D, and this means that subsequently most development expenses are allowable against income and the owner's tax rates are effectively reduced. Net income from timber sales are taxed similarly.

What would happen if an investor chooses to invest in woodland by means of a Woodland Trust ownership scheme (as an alternative to investing direct), and elects to be taxed under Schedule D, is shown in the following worked example. Normally Woodland Trust co-ownership schemes are formed to plant woodland on bare land and comprise about 1,000 acres. Twenty shares are normally issued in each Trust and each investor can buy the number of shares best suited to his particular needs. It is assumed in the example below, which is provided by the Economic Forestry Group, that woodland development takes place over five years.

Worked example of investment in woodlands through co-ownership

Outlay

Cost of share in Woodland Trust £4,000

This £4,000 covers the cost of buying the land, preliminary expenses. No tax relief is available.

Establishment costs over 5 years per share

Capital	£2,600
Revenue	£6,000
Total establishment costs	£8,600

Relief available

For the investor subject to the top rate of tax at 83%:

During the first 5 years relief would be	£5,843
On deferred capital claims over the next 6 years relief would be	£1,295
Total relief	£7,138

Thus, the net cost of development to the investor is £8,600 less £7,138=£1,462.

The objective of the above worked example is to show how to create a fund of capital out of income that would otherwise be paid away in tax, by using forestry grants and relief of income tax on development expenditure. Grants are calculated on the basis of £18 per acre, which is the current level of planting grant, while costs include all development operations such as planting, putting in roads, fencing and management.

Thus, for the investment of £4,000 plus a net cost of development of £1,462 after tax relief, the high tax payer has translated his depreciating cash into an asset of 50 acres of woodland for £5,462 – or £109 per acre. In addition to boosting his after-tax income considerably as a result of the offsettable reliefs available, he has the prospect of income from the felled timber to come, plus an appreciating asset in the form of his 50 acres.

CAPITAL TAXES

No capital gains tax liability occurs on the disposal of growing timber, but an assessment will be made on any gains realised on the disposal of the land unless such disposal occurs on death.

Capital transfer tax is the area which provides most benefit to woodland owners. Following the modifications to capital transfer tax as far as it affected woodlands, made in the 1976 Finance Act, the situation relating to all transfers after 6 April 1976 is that reliefs for businesses are applicable to the owner of commercial woodlands assessed for income under either Schedule B or Schedule D. Alternatively there are special provisions following death available to individuals which permit the deferment of tax on growing timber. There are a number of important exemptions for woodland owners so far as capital transfer tax is concerned. These include transfers between husband and wife up to any value, the first £15,000 of value transferred by any individual, life-time transfers of £2,000 annually for any individual and regular gifts ranking as normal expenditure out of income.

If woodlands managed on a commercial basis are handed over by way of gift during the lifetime of the investor, and if the woodlands have been owned for at least two out of the five years preceding the transfer then tax is charged at the lower life-time rates, provided the investor handing them over survives a further three years. Both land and trees handed over by the investor qualify for 'business assets relief', which reduces the value transferred by 30 per cent. The tax on the reduced amount of liability can be paid in instalments, spread over eight years, and interest will only be added to outstanding instalments from the date their payment is due.

The Finance Act 1975 recognised the importance of forestry and made special provisions in the case of individuals for deferment of tax on growing timber for transfers on death. The value of the growing timber can then be left out of account for tax purposes and no liability to tax on the growing timber will occur until it is disposed of by sale or life-time transfer. Expenses of disposal, felling and replanting may be allowed against the net value of a disposal for capital transfer tax purposes.

Chapter 24

The Investment Attractions of Going 'Non-Resident'

The names of those who have quit these shores to increase their after-tax income reads like *Who's Who*. Tony Jacklin, Jackie Stewart, Sean Connery, Rod Stewart, Sue Barker, Frederick Forsyth, Michael Caine... the list seems almost endless. The whole point of the exercise is to move your base to an overseas point which offers you greater opportunities to keep more of what you make, whether in the form of earned or unearned income, and which is also pleasant to live in. That latter point is important, because some countries may offer decided tax advantages but may not be all that attractive to live in. Albania, for example, has no income tax but one rarely hears of a tax exile heading for that forbidding country, even if they should get permission to enter. You could, of course, move to somewhere like the Cayman Islands, but the relatively small population and somewhat claustrophobic international banking environment is hardly the place for a balanced family life. Even in Jersey, Guernsey or the Isle of Man (the use of which by UK residents is the subject of the next chapter) the attractions are limited in that the Channel Islands resident, while being liable to income tax at only 20p in the pound (and no capital gains tax whatsoever) is caught by capital transfer tax if he or she moved there after the end of 1974. Another disadvantage to Jersey is that the island has the world's highest ratio of cars to road space. Do not forget, either, that you do lose a certain amount of 'psychological income' by leaving Britain and living elsewhere. Many an expatriate soon forgets the strikes, the taxes, the fog and rain, and pines for the cosy

166

British pub or for a view of the Downs on a clear day. Some come back.

Emotions apart, the advantages that the non-resident gets from achieving that status is that he or she does not pay tax on foreign income or on capital gains, so far as the UK tax authorities are concerned anyway. This leaves the non-resident to settle his affairs with the tax authority of the country of his choice, and if he wants to invest in Britain – say by buying gilts – he can claim back the withholding tax. Since 24 March 1977 all issues of gilts have had interest paid to non-residents net of withholding tax; on issues before this date, the tax situation varies from one gilt to another. This claw-back facility exists as long as there is a double taxation agreement between the UK and the expatriate's new country of residence.

THE EXCHANGE CONTROL REGULATIONS

Before going non-resident, it is necessary to understand the UK Exchange Control Regulations and also the workings of the investment currency market. The Exchange Control Act 1947 (explained in chapter 8) is the basis for all the British exchange control rules and guidelines.

What the exchange regulations add up to is that, from the investment viewpoint, UK private investors tend to be locked into UK shares and gilts if they seek a combination of capital gain and income. If the investment currency premium has moved down substantially – it was over 80 per cent, effectively, not so very long ago – then the investor in overseas shares loses out because he will have paid the high premium and recoups the low premium when he sells. And he is subject to capital gains tax on top. As you will appreciate, because of the premium, the private investor has to look for pretty spectacular gains from direct investment in overseas shares before the exercise is worthwhile. Of course, such an investor can buy units in an overseas-oriented unit trust or shares in an overseas-oriented investment trust, but in the case of the unit trust he has to suffer a loss of something of the order of 5 per cent in 'front-end loading' and his capital investment is out of his own control. And on what basis do you select such a trust? Looking at the 1977 performance tables produced for unit trusts by *Planned Savings,* of the bottom five performers, three were specialists in North America and were caught out by the 1977 Wall Street fall while the other two were invested in the Far East.

Thus, apart from the massive tax advantages, the non-resident gains substantially because he can diversify his investment portfolio (depending on the exchange control regulations of his country of choice) without these formidable hurdles.

THE MECHANICS OF GOING NON-RESIDENT

You become a non-resident by signing a declaration to the effect that it is your intention to reside in a country outside the Scheduled Territories for at least three years. Bear firmly in mind that such re-designation for exchange control purposes does not affect your freedom to visit the UK whenever you like for periods of up to six months a year. Basically you are treated as a British resident if you stay in this country for 183 days or more in any British tax year. You are also treated as resident if your visits average 90 days or more a year taking four consecutive years together. But if you have somewhere in the UK available for occupation – even if it is only a room in someone else's house – then a visit to Britain of one day only can make you a resident for tax purposes. The one exception to this last rule is where you have a full-time occupation abroad.

The Scheduled Territories referred to consist of the UK, including the Channel Islands and the Isle of Man, the Republic of Ireland (special tax exemption for writers and artists here) and Gibraltar (income tax of 40 per cent, death duties of up to a maximum of 20 per cent). Exchange control regulations do not apply to transactions between individuals resident in the Scheduled Territories. However, such regulations do apply with respect to the rest of the world, which for exchange control purposes is divided, like Caesar's Gaul, into three parts. There are the Overseas Sterling Area countries, the EEC and the rest of the world.

The essential point about these divisions is that the whereabouts of your country of destination determines how much you can take with you when you quit these shores and how much you have to leave behind you for a further four years until you can transfer your capital to your chosen country without paying the investment currency premium. If you wanted to take up residence in one of the countries of the Overseas Sterling Area before 1977 you could transfer, at the time of going to live in your country of destination, £20,000 for family unit (husband, wife and children under eighteen). If you wanted to go and live anywhere else, the allowance would be a paltry £5,000 per family unit unless you were aged sixty-five for men and sixty for women in which case you could transfer up to £20,000.

On 26 October 1977, in Mr Healey's mini-budget, the Chancellor decided that these strictures required some loosening in the light of inflation. He upped the amount of currency you can take with you, free of the investment currency premium, from £20,000 to £40,000 for those going to Overseas Sterling Area countries, but left the £5,000 ceiling still in being for those going anywhere else. He also maintained the four-year restriction on the transfer of any remaining capital assets in excess of £40,000 or £5,000 respectively – unless you choose to pay the investment currency premium.

LOOPHOLES

Apart from lugging along an elderly relative, which increases your allowance from £5,000 to £40,000 if you are going to a country outside the Overseas Sterling Area (the funds, by the way, can be moved out up to one month in advance of your move), you can have a go at trying to prove financial hardship and, if you are successful, you will be allowed to take more out. If you are legally separated, both you and your wife are entitled to apply for separate emigration allowances, which would have the effect of doubling the amount of capital which you and your estranged spouse can take out of the country. In theory, at least, you and your wife could re-unite at some happy trysting spot in the South of France or the Canary Islands.

You can take out £300 in foreign currency and £100 in

sterling plus all your household goods, personal effects and your own car or cars. These items are not deducted from the capital transfer allowance. So, if you have a houseful of small but valuable objets d'art such as stamps, coins, non-listed paintings, jewellery, antiques, ceramics (all of which command an international market price) among your household goods, then this is one way of exporting capital without exceeding the legal limit. Equally, you may be able to take out a couple of Rolls Royces as your family cars. But be warned, evidence of a dramatic change in lifestyle immediately before you go non-resident will raise the official hackles. Build up to the move gradually.

Another loophole is provided by the use of life and endowment policies, as long as they are not linked with a unit trust and have been taken out three years before you go. Any capital resulting from these policies can be sent to a non-resident during the four-year capital restriction period without taking anything away from the basic allowance and without attracting the investment currency premium.

You can use your restricted UK capital to raise money in your new country, and without paying the premium. Your UK bank will arrange (using your UK capital as collateral) to guarantee your overseas bankers and so enable you to borrow foreign currency from them so that you can buy a home.

Your restricted capital can be invested in UK stocks and shares and income arising from this can be used to pay for your visits to the UK during the four years of restriction, for premiums on your insurance policies and for school fees if you have children at UK schools. By the way, you can still claim part of your UK personal allowances to offset your UK taxation when you are non-resident.

CAPITAL TRANSFER TAX

As far as capital transfer tax is concerned, the Inland Revenue now requires that the emigrant both changes residence and lives overseas for at least three years (short holidays disregarded) before transfers to other individuals escape CTT. Since November 1974 residence in the Channel Islands or Isle of Man does not qualify as 'abroad' in the context of CTT.

If you happen to be a foreigner, Section 45 of the 1974 Finance Act hits you hard if you have worked in the UK for many years and still regard your country of origin as 'home'. Once you have spent seventeen out of twenty tax years in the UK, any transfers made (not necessarily in the UK) become liable to CTT in the UK.

THOSE EMPLOYED ABROAD

Since the Budget in March 1977 the Chancellor has provided four main branches of tax relief for those at 'the sharp end of exporting'. First, the individual employed by a UK company who is sent abroad for 30 days or more, whether continuous or not, in a fiscal year is taxable on only 75 per cent of his earnings for the foreign duties. These foreign earnings are calculated from the proportion of the year spent abroad. Second, this relief is extended to seafarers and aircrew whose voyages or flights start or end (but not start and end) in the UK. Third, an individual who works abroad for a foreign company, all his duties for that company being performed out of the UK, gets the same exemption on 25 per cent of his earnings from that employment regardless of the time he spends abroad. Finally, this last individual is not taxed on his travel costs.

The problem the Chancellor faced in providing this relief was caused by the 1974 legislation which substantially re-wrote the law on taxation of UK residents working abroad. Two favoured groups were then created. The first remains undisturbed and consists of individuals who are resident, but who are abroad for a continuous period of 365 days. They are wholly exempt from UK tax on earnings and on re-imbursed expenses. It was the second category, those who were given a 25 per cent tax exemption under the 1974 legislation, which the Chancellor cleared up in his 1977 Budget. The two pieces of legislation – 1974 and 1977 – taken together mean that if you are absent for a total of 365 days (less 62 days allowed for visits back to Britain) then all your UK earnings are free of British income tax. Where you are away for at least 30 days, in total, each year then, broadly, 25 per cent of the earnings for that period are free of UK tax. So, if you earn

171

£9,000 from UK employment abroad and spend 60 days out of the country working abroad, then one-sixth of your salary attracts the 25 per cent deductions, which adds up to a meagre £375. Normally you would be far better off engineering a separate contract of employment, in addition to your UK contract of employment, with an overseas subsidiary of the group you happen to work for. Such a contract has to have all the features of a 'real' contract of employment (sickness, holiday entitlements and the rest), otherwise the Revenue will not accept it. But the astute executive who works for a group with overseas subsidiaries or affiliates can considerably increase his after-tax income by the use of a separate overseas contract.

HIDDEN PITFALLS

Returning to the non-residents who permanently move their domicile elsewhere, it is worth pointing out that there are hidden pitfalls laid for the unwary. If exchange controls are dismantled, and if the investment currency premium disappears, you then lose any premium you may have paid earlier, for example on the purchase of property overseas when you were still resident in the UK. There are other pitfalls also: people buying property in Spain, for example, should know that in order to reduce certain tax liabilities, a substantially lower purchase price than that actually to be paid is sometimes proposed by local agents or Spanish lawyers for inclusions in the property deed. If the property is then later sold, the Spanish authorities may then allow only the false, lower amount to be sent back to the UK, leaving the balance in Spain. Another case is that of Greece which opposes any ownership of property by foreigners, while France does not allow local borrowing arrangements to finance house purchase. So your dream in the sun could turn into something of a nightmare unless you check everything out well beforehand. The old adage 'a stitch in time' holds particularly true.

Chapter 25

Using the Off-Shore Tax Havens

Let it be said at the outset that Jersey does not like to be
known as an 'off-shore tax haven': it prefers the title of 'off-
shore financial centre'. 'Jersey' is used for convenience in this
chapter, as a catch-all title and example for all Britain's off-
shore tax havens, which encompass Guernsey, Alderney, Sark
and the Isle of Man. The reason why Jersey figures so prom-
inently is that the financial structure and infrastructure which
is necessary to any financial centre is primarily located on
Jersey in the crowded streets of St Helier. In this port all the
British clearing banks, principal merchant banks, some secondary banks, lawyers, accountants, tax advisers jostle with
each other for representation, as do the big firms of City of
London money brokers. There are in the region of 10,000
'brass plate companies' registered in St Helier and there can
be few large British companies, and few private individuals
with substantial investment portfolios, who do not make use
of the facilities offered in St Helier.

Not that Jersey advertises such facilities. The approach is
circuitous. A company or an individual needs substantial assets
to arrange the 'right' introductions. So the preliminary vetting
can be carried out at a merchant bank or a City of London
solicitor's office on the UK mainland before the letters of
introduction are written to Jersey branch offices or to Jersey
solicitors or accountants.

The opportunities available on Jersey are particularly attractive if you happen to be:

(a) going non-resident and needing to find a 'home' for your
    sterling assets which are restricted for the four years after

173

you take up your foreign domicile (unless you wish to pay the investment currency premium);
(b) an employee of a British company working abroad, or a UK resident working abroad for an overseas company;
(c) building up a private company and have potential tax threats from the future disposal of your shares on the horizon; or
(d) non-resident but wish to use Jersey as a secure financial centre (the Jersey banking system being under the control of the Bank of England) for the disposition of your investment portfolio in and outside the UK.

JERSEY AND CAPITAL TRANSFER TAX

First, rid yourself of the idea that the following pages are going to be devoted to the attractions of moving to Jersey as a resident. To start with, Jersey allows in a mere trickle of UK citizens, and these are subject to a wealth assessment criterion. Second, and more important, much of the gilt has been taken off the gingerbread of being a Jersey resident by Clause 43(c) of the Finance Act 1975, which singled out the Channel Islands and the Isle of Man for special treatment as far as capital transfer tax is concerned. Under this provision a UK resident who became domiciled in the off-shore islands after 10 December 1974 is deemed to be still living permanently in Britain for capital transfer tax purposes. The reason why the Treasury did this, despite determined hostility from the islands' financial communities, was that the Channel Islands and the Isle of Man were considered to be special cases because of their geographical proximity and because they were within the UK exchange control area. These factors had made them 'a ready escape route in the past' and they would become 'all the more advantageous' with the introduction of CTT. Those quotes were from Joel Barnett, Chief Secretary to the Treasury at that time. The islands' reply was that they were no more accessible from the UK than were many parts of Belgium, France, Holland or the Irish Republic and that someone moving to the Continent had only to wait four years before laying his hands on his sterling assets.

However, the British Government's target was not the

expatriate. Its target was spelled out by Joel Barnett: 'It has been possible for wealthy men to use the islands as a base from which to retain overall direction of substantial private business enterprises without in law having a domicile in the United Kingdom.' This was an argument that the islands could not dispute because there were many well-known instances in recent years of ostensible 'settlers' being heavily involved in mainland business and even commuting several times a week.

So, quite apart from the restrictions on the number of wealthy individuals allowed to settle in Jersey, the fact that the off-shore islands are caught in the CTT net reduces the attractions of the 20 per cent income tax – a rate of tax which was set in 1940 and has remained unaltered since – and the attractions of nil capital gains tax. However, the flourishing financial community in St Helier does not depend to a significant extent on wealthy islanders as the vast proportion of its income is derived from those living outside the islands who wish to use the island as a financial base, and from companies using the island for tax-saving reasons: remember that the off-shore islands offer all the security of the British banking system and that, in turn, provides peace of mind. Although other tax havens could provide higher benefits they may not, if they are not regulated by a recognised central bank, offer the same peace of mind. In addition, all the facilities exist in the islands for carrying out the most complex financial and legal transactions throughout the world, facilities which may not exist elsewhere.

INCOME TAX COMPANY VERSUS CORPORATION TAX COMPANY

In the pedantic words of Jersey legalese, the 'commonly operated legal structures' in Jersey include Jersey-registered companies comprising trading companies and investment holding or dealing companies; Jersey-registered companies controlled outside Jersey; partnerships; discretionary trusts. You can, of course, use more than one of these in any one operation, but it is essential to distinguish between the trading, or income tax, companies and the companies controlled outside Jersey.

The first category in the list above – Jersey-registered companies involved in trading, or created to hold or deal in

175

investments – is liable to income tax at the standard rate of 20 per cent. Trading companies can be formed on behalf of a non-Jersey resident either for trading within the island or for handling trading transactions to and from external sources. Such a company has obvious benefits for a UK holding company because the Jersey subsidiary can carry out, for example, re-invoicing operations. To take one instance, a UK company seeking to break into a new overseas market would 'sell in' the equipment (on paper) to Jersey and then 'sell on' the same equipment overseas (also on paper). Profits earned by the Jersey company would be subject to the 20 per cent income tax rate, and the UK company could choose at which time, from a tax planning point of view, profits built up in the Jersey subsidiary should be repatriated. While the Jersey company is liable to the 20 per cent tax, there is no profits tax, corporation tax (in the UK sense) or capital gains tax. Such a company can also be used for distribution of cash flows from a high-tax area to a low-tax area by the manipulation of such devices as management fees, patents and royalties. The investment holding company can be formed by a person resident and domiciled in Jersey and can hold investments through such a company anywhere in the world.

Investment dealing companies, as the name suggests, are primarily formed to deal in investments; the dealing profits, less losses, as well as investment income, are subject to income tax at 20 per cent. There are a number of these operations structured by merchant banks to invest in the money markets, in commodities and in equities which enable a UK resident to translate highly-taxed income into capital gain which is passed back to the UK resident free of capital gains tax. One merchant bank, for example, constructed a commodity dealing company in Jersey through which high-income earners could buy units in a trust. The income from the cash invested on the money markets (a risk-free investment) was then used to take positions in certain commodities, managed by a UK commodity broker. Profits earned from commodity dealing through the Jersey company attracted no capital gains tax as Jersey has no such tax. The increase in the value of the units was thus received by the unit holder free of capital gains tax while the income from invested cash pooled up in Jersey was subject to only the

20 per cent income tax liability. There are a number of such schemes in operation which are designed to make full use of Jersey's advantages where the high-income UK-resident is concerned.

If participation in a Jersey trading company is required by an individual who is outside the sterling area (in essence, the UK, the Isle of Man, the Channel Islands, the Republic of Ireland and Gibraltar), Bank of England permission is necessary. Formation of such a company takes about three weeks to a month. When exchange control permission is required (for dealing in currencies other then sterling) formation is likely to take a period of months. The control and administration of such a company must be exercised in Jersey although there is no general bar covering the nationality of directors, of which there must be at least three, each holding a minimum of three shares of £1 each. Directors' and General Meetings must be held on the island of Jersey. A registered office must be held on the island and an annual return of shareholders must be made to the Judicial Greffier of the island (a return which is available for public inspection).

The alternative type of company structure is the 'Corporation Tax' company, so called because such a company pays corporation tax of a maximum of £300 each year irrespective of the amount of profits the company earns. Such a company must be controlled outside Jersey, and by control the Jersey authorities mean directors' rather than shareholders' control. The residence of the individual directors, who must be at least three in number, does not determine the company's place of control, but the Jersey Comptroller of Income Tax will normally accept that the control of the company is outside Jersey if the beneficial owner of the company lives outside Jersey and outside the UK, if the management of the company is carried on outside Jersey and if the directors' meetings are held in the country of control. Such strictures are the reason why little groups of sober-suited businessmen can be seen in the hotels and restaurants of Dinard, an easy hydrofoil ride from Jersey, huddled round tables, rustling through papers and ticking off points on their respective agendas while they clock up fifty or sixty board meetings of Jersey-located corporation tax companies at a time. The little groups are composed of one Jersey

177

resident (normally an employee of a Jersey Bank or Trust Company) and two non-UK (and non-Jersey) residents.

The chief advantages of having such a company is that it pays corporation tax of £300 per annum irrespective of the level of profits made, and no accounts have to be filed with the Jersey authorities. If the company's ultimate place of control is in a country which has no tax, then the £300 corporation tax paid would be the only tax suffered. The owner of the company has the additional advantage of the security of dealing within the British banking system.

For both the 'income tax company' and the 'corporation tax company' formation time is about the same, three to four weeks unless exchange control permission is required from the Bank of England. Costs of establishing a Jersey-registered company are dependent on scale fees payable according to the amount of authorised capital, but the smallest company with a capital of £100 and with a normal Memorandum and Articles of Association would cost about £200–£300 to form. While the control of such a company belongs to the benefical owner in the case of the corporation tax company, the administration of such a company or of a trading (or income tax) company would normally be carried out by a bank or trust company in St Helier. Such financial organisations would charge about £400 to £600 per annum for maintaining a registered office and a modicum of services. Probably the cheapest method of constructing such a company is through one of the Jersey branches of a clearing bank's trust company. All the clearing bank trust companies have extensive Jersey networks, as have the bigger merchant banks, although the merchant banks would prove slightly more expensive than the clearing banks.

THE INLAND REVENUE

The UK Inland Revenue is somewhat vexed by the fact that it cannot find out about UK residents with Channel Islands accounts. (It is not, of course, bothered about the affairs of non-UK residents.) Anybody can fly to the islands with a suitcase full of cash and deposit it with any number of leading banks and keep quiet about the interest quietly accumulating. However, the island's banks are equally worried, since capital transfer tax was extended to the Channel Islands and the Isle of Man, that they should not give cause for grievance to the UK Inland Revenue which would tempt the UK Treasury to extend its encroachments into the financial affairs of the islands. About subsidiary companies established for trading purposes by UK companies the Inland Revenue is fairly relaxed. After all, the average member of the British public, and certainly the left wing of the Labour Party, does not understand the use to which these companies are put, and there is virtually no publicity about them. It is a nice cosy little set-up and, as far as the UK Inland Revenue authorities are concerned, the establishment of a Jersey-registered trading company, paying income tax in Jersey, is perfectly acceptable as long as such an arrangement does not involve the transfer of part of the UK company's business in order to mitigate its UK tax position.

For UK private individuals the position is vastly different. Before capital transfer tax was extended to Jersey (but only affecting transactions after December 1974), wealthy families could escape the old-style estate duty, which was a voluntary tax anyway, by creating discretionary trusts of labyrinthine complexity, trusts which could last eighty years. These trusts were often controlled by a corporation tax company so that the income and capital gains arising from trust funds could be pooled into the company and attract the bare minimum of tax (once £100, now £300). The advent of CTT to the islands has removed the rationale for creating such trusts as they now come under the CTT net.

THE USES TO WHICH YOU CAN PUT JERSEY

First, going non-resident. This in turn can be split into two parts. The first part concerns the use to which you can put your sterling assets for the four-year period of restrictions before you can transfer them to your new country of residence free of the investment currency premium. If you are astute enough and wealthy enough, you can create a corporation tax company in Jersey through which your sterling assets can be deployed in stocks and shares and in commodities, or on the money markets if you want absolute security. This means the income plus capital gains on your Jersey-based assets will pile up free of capital gains tax, and subject only to the £300 per annum corporation tax. This device can also be used by UK residents working wholly abroad. Equally you may wish, after you have gone non-resident for over four years and have transferred your cash elsewhere, still to deploy some or all of your assets through the UK banking system for security reasons. You can create a corporation tax company to deal in investments in Jersey and apply for exchange control permission to deal in foreign currencies. This will allow you to deploy your resources throughout the world, to manipulate currencies to your benefit and to deal in the London, New York, Frankfurt or Tokyo stock exchanges. The income and capital gain arising from such deployment would, again, be subject to the maximum corporation tax of £300 a year plus the administration costs of running such a company and you would have no further tax liability if the country of your domicile imposes no tax upon you.

Another use to which a Jersey company can be put would considerably increase the wealth of an entrepreneur who is busily engaged in building up a private company in the UK and who has the long-term intention of going non-resident. Let's imagine you are a businessman who has worked for twenty years to build up a private company which is now worth a couple of million pounds. If you sell the shares or go public (the latter is a much less likely choice nowadays), then you attract very hefty capital gains tax liabilities on the build-up in the value of the shares. Let's suppose, however, that at the end of the company's first year you had decided that some time in the future you and your family would leave the UK and domicile yourselves elsewhere. You can create a Jersey trust and sell the shares of the private company to the trust. The sale would incur capital gains tax at the end of the company's first year, but the subsequent build-up in the value of the company would be pooled into the Jersey trust with no eventual liability to future UK capital gains tax. Through the facility of the trust you would be building up wealth free of capital gains tax. The settlor of a Jersey discretionary trust need not be a Jersey resident but the trustees must be. The beneficiaries of the trust would be the widow and children of the settlor or anybody so nominated – other then a Jersey resident, that is. The discretionary trust can hold the shares of the UK company directly or indirectly, for example through a Jersey corporation tax company. The income from the shares and the build-up in their value can be accumulated during the whole period of the trust at the discretion of the trustees. Disposal of an interest under the settlement can be effected, free of capital gains tax, by 'selling' the interest in the discretionary trust to a Jersey trust company.

There are two provisos to this scheme. One is that you must eventually go non-resident because the trust assets will be subject to capital transfer tax (CTT is levied annually on foreign trusts) until they are transferred to your new country of domicile. The other is that you will need specialist advice on the highly complex Section 478, Income and Corporation Taxes Act 1970.

Bear in mind also that it is more difficult to get money out of the trust than it is to inject cash: it is easier for the individual building up a fortune than for the individual who already has one. As far as the sale is concerned, a number of Jersey trust companies have schemes which are tailored to extract money from the trust to your benefit. For example, the trust company could tailor-make a scheme with a Jersey discretionary trust (which it may have been administering) under which the trust company is appointed contingent beneficiary, say fourteen days hence. Let's suppose that the value of the trust's assets is £100,000. The beneficial interest in the trust can be sold to the trust company for, say, £95,000, the missing £5,000 representing the trust company's turn for arranging the deal. It is important to bear in mind that such a disposal of an interest under a settlement is, of course, excluded from capital gains tax.

Another example of the successful use of a corporation tax company – this one is for the wealthy sea-lover – is its use by a British expatriate yacht owner who wishes to fly the British flag. A corporation tax company can be created to own the yacht in Jersey. The yacht itself, bought free of customs duty or VAT, can never actually come into Jersey or into any UK port without attracting both customs duty and VAT (which would be payable when the yacht entered a UK harbour and is reclaimable as the vessel sails out) but it can fly the British flag in its snug Mediterranean berth. One slight difference with a corporation tax company set up to own a yacht is that the company's board meetings must be held inside the UK (the tiny island of Sark being the favourite spot for such meetings) in order to retain British registration. Even the £300 corporation tax is reclaimable if the yacht owning company can satisfy the Jersey Comptroller of Income Tax that no income tax would be payable if the company were resident in Jersey.

Lastly, you can create a corporation tax investment-holding company in Jersey so that you can swap shares in a UK private company for the investment-holding company shares in Jersey, thus avoiding capital gains tax on such a share disposal. But bear in mind that this popular scheme, which resulted in many a British businessman controlling his business empire from Jersey at an enormous tax benefit, gave rise to the capital transfer tax attack on Jersey in the first place.

INDEX